Monday Morning Mail

Scott Kronick

Published by
Alain Charles Asia Publishing Ltd.
University House
11-13 Lower Grosvenor Place,
London SW1W 0EX, UK
Tel: +44 (0)20 7834 7676
Fax: +44 (0)20 7973 0076
E-mail: info@alaincharlesasia.com
Web: www.alaincharlesasia.com
Beijing Office
Tel: +86(0)10 8472 1250
Fax: +86(0)10 5885 0639
Written by Scott Kronick,
CEO of Ogilvy Public Relations, Asia Pacific
Edited by Martin Savery, ACA Publishing Ltd

ALL RIGHTS RESERVED. NO PART OF THIS
PUBLICATION MAY BE REPRODUCED IN MATERIAL FORM,
BY ANY MEANS, WHETHER GRAPHIC,
ELECTRONIC, MECHANICAL OR OTHER, INCLUDING
PHOTOCOPYING OR INFORMATION STORAGE, IN WHOLE OR IN PART,
AND MAY NOT BE USED TO PREPARE OTHER PUBLICATIONS WITHOUT
WRITTEN PERMISSION FROM THE PUBLISHER.

The greatest care has been taken to ensure accuracy but the
publisher can accept no responsibility for errors or omissions, or
for any liability occasioned by relying on its content.

ISBN: 978-1-910760-01-7

A catalogue record for Monday Morning Mail is available from the
National Bibliographic Service of the British Library.

Contents

Foreword iv

So It Begins 1

People 3

Organization 29

Leadership 59

Client Service 72

Big Picture 107

Learning 126

Relationships 137

Winning 145

Responsibility 166

Conclusion 171

Glossary 172

Foreword

In my 30 years of working in public relations, one of the biggest challenges I have faced is making sure everyone is informed of everything that is going on. I have worked under some of the very best leaders in our industry. Miles Young, Marcia Silverman, Paul Heath, TB Song, Shenan Chuang, Ruby Fu, Matthew Anderson, Chris Graves, Steve Dahllof, Stuart Smith, to name a few. At Ogilvy & Mather, we are blessed with strong leadership, people who genuinely care about the future of the industry and developing talent to define the future.

Ogilvy & Mather is often called the University of Marketing and I understand why. We have some of the smartest people working with us who develop a treasure trove of great thinking; golden nuggets disguised as presentations, viewpoints, articles and more. If they sit in the email boxes of just a few people, they are worthless. When they are shared amongst the broader Ogilvy population, they become the currency that makes up true market leadership.

With the *Monday Morning Mail* I have tried to share the wisdom shared with me since I started in this business with all of my colleagues. I have also used the *Monday Morning Mail* to share my own particular views on the world in an effort to reach as many people in our organization as possible. I have wanted them to hear from me personally what I believe is right and wrong, what we need to do to succeed and how to avoid failure. There is also the schmaltzy passage here and there that just talks about life.

I have collected these passages over a seven-year period and decided to print them for all of the new and old staff as a reference for where we have come from and where we are headed. I hope you enjoy the read.

I am hugely grateful to my wife Lisa who has sat beside me on weekends as I typed away on the computer. Lisa is the most loving and caring partner I could ever imagine, and I credit her with the great luck and fortune I have had with my career. My kids, Jacquelin and Samuel, also deserve credit. They are both brilliant in their own way and I have learned a ton from them. My father and mother also gave me a great foundation and feature in many of the passages. I have them too to thank.

Toni Zhou, my assistant for nearly a decade, is brilliant. She should be credited with translating my mails every other Monday for the staff's consumption. Nita Wang also deserves thanks as she joined recently and has helped with the translation for the Chinese edition. The brilliant Liu Haiming, a great friend and one of the best translators and cultural interpreters I have ever met in China, I owe much to. He organized this book and helped to polish both the English and Chinese. Finally, my special thanks to Ying Mathieson and Martin Savery of ACA Publishing who, once again, agreed to publish this tribute, and to Jon Medwick, who was kind enough to help with the illustrations.

David Ogilvy was famous for writing, "if each of us hire people who are smaller than we are, we will become a company of dwarfs. But if each of us hire people who are bigger than we are, we will become a company of giants."

I want to thank the giants of this company who I have worked with for so many years, who have made me one of the smallest people in Ogilvy. This *Monday Morning Mail* compilation is for you.

Onwards and upwards.

So It Begins

Joy in filing the *Monday Morning Mail* every week.

Chapter One

So it Begins

And so it begins… May 12, 2008

We're 88 days away from the opening ceremonies (of the Beijing Olympics) and counting.

In an effort to communicate more often with the entire Ogilvy PR network, I plan to write to you regularly with updates on what is taking place at Ogilvy PR throughout our China-Hong Kong offices. In these notes I plan to share cases and resources more regularly.

In terms of our year-to-date performance, we are collectively continuing our record of delivering strong numbers and, like every May, we have seven months to close our new business gaps in all offices. The challenge is not small ... but it is attainable and I have the confidence. In the spirit of our wonderful client adidas, "Impossible is Nothing."

A few facts about us:

Ogilvy PR in China-Hong Kong is made up of 458 people. We have eight offices overall:

  Ogilvy PR: *Beijing/Shanghai/Guangzhou/Hong Kong*
  H-Line Ogilvy: *Beijing/Shanghai/Guangzhou*
  iPR: *Hong Kong*

Our Direction

Our goal for this year is to create influential, industry-leading campaigns that build our clients' business, demonstrate our influence and insight with a strong idea at the center and to develop and drive campaigns that are talked about.

We will accomplish this through our practice specialization (which is consistent with our regional strategy), through talent development and by networking, both inside China-Hong Kong, throughout the region and together with the Ogilvy PR Network and Ogilvy Group globally.

I hope you will all embrace this direction to ensure we are the leading communications company in this region!

People

In the PR business, the team is really what matters most.

Chapter Two

People

A nice place to work, July 28, 2008

Good morning colleagues,

One of my favorite passages from David Ogilvy's "The Unpublished David Ogilvy" is on Corporate Culture...

"Dear Bill:

You have asked me to describe our corporate culture as I see it.

Corporate culture is a compound of many things - tradition, mythology, ritual, customs, habits, heroes, peculiarities, and values. Here is how I see our culture:

A Nice Place To Work

Some of our people spend their entire working lives in our agency. We do our damnedest to make it a happy experience. I put this first, believing that superior service to our clients, and profits for our stockholders, depends on it.

We treat our people like human beings. We help when they are in trouble - with their jobs, with illness, with alcoholism, and so on.

We help our people make the best of their talents. We invest an awful lot of time and money in training - perhaps more than any of our competitors.

Our system of management is singularly democratic. We don't like hierarchical bureaucracy or rigid pecking orders.

We abhor ruthlessness.

We give our executives an extraordinary degree of freedom and independence.

People

We like people with gentle manners. Our New York office goes so far as to give an annual award for 'professionalism combined with civility.' The Jules Fine Award, named after the first winner.

We like people who are honest. Honest in argument, honest with clients, honest with suppliers, honest with the company – and, above all, honest with consumers."

David goes on, but you get the picture. I certainly hope all of you feel this way about our culture in China and work to create such an environment for us in China.

This Week's Highlights

We pretty much started the week in Beijing and Shanghai helping a client with a crisis, and we ended the week with another potential crisis on the horizon. In the middle of the week, I was also called in on a very special issue with one company related to the Olympics. To a greater or lesser extent, our firm is serving as counsel to clients on a number of highly sensitive issues. This makes me extremely proud because we have a number of clients who confide in us and turn to us for help in addressing some of the more sensitive business issues in China. Our crisis capabilities are certainly growing and we are becoming more adept at handling these. In my experience, crises are the moments of truth when your clients really depend on you, and these are the times you must step up your game to show your clients that you care as much as they do and resolving the issue is of top priority.

Many of us were also heavily involved in creating the case studies for the Ogilvy PR Professional Service Awards Competition. I certainly hope we win some of these, but of much more importance is for us to have the cases. All of us must improve our ability to think strategically about our clients' business and I find writing these case studies is a great discipline in really focusing our thinking on the business/communications problems we are trying to solve for our clients. My thanks to all of you who are contributing to the development of this year's cases.

I was also involved in an exciting Olympic initiative that will be introduced to you all very soon. Certainly Ogilvy wants to exit the 2008 Olympics as the most "rooted" firm in China, and we had a brainstorm that arrived at an idea that we will introduce in the next few weeks. Stay tuned.

With five months left in 2008, we need to focus on finishing this year strong and setting ourselves up for success in 2009. We'll begin the 2009 budget process very soon, and I hope you are all thinking about the future of your teams, your own professional life and where we want to take the business in the new year.

Monday Morning Mail

> ### Environmental Tip of the Week
>
> Turn off the water faucet while you are brushing your teeth. The average bathroom faucet flows at a rate of two gallons per minute. Turning off the tap while brushing your teeth in the morning and at bedtime can save up to 8 gallons of water per day, which equals 240 gallons a month!

****

Dare to dream, dream big and go big or go home! September 8, 2008

Dear Friends,

Life seems to be getting back to normal. For me, this last week was packed with meetings of clients wanting to re-ignite their communications after the Olympic hiatus. That's good news and can solve a lot of my post-Olympic depression. It was truly a fantastic three weeks and for me a wonderful eight-year lead up.

With the Olympics past and the paralympics beginning, I encourage you all to take time to think about your own dreams. My mom had a saying: "Dream Big and Go Big or Go Home". I think part of all of our personal plans should be to set some personal dreams and chase them. And not to let anyone stand in your way of achieving these. I am sure participating in the Olympics for many of the past week's Olympians was a dream come true. And for this week's paralympians, even more so. For those in Beijing or visiting Beijing, I hope you will take time out to watch a game or two. And I hope all of you take time out to dream.

This Past Week

For me, this past week was characterized by a number of conversations. Some fascinating and eye-opening and some a waste of time. But I am glad to have had these. As I walked through our offices in Beijing and Shanghai I can clearly see how busy we are. But I hope this doesn't prohibit human interaction. Emailing people sitting next to you a message that could be communicated should be prohibited. We are in the communications business and often emails don't convey feelings... they don't smile nor laugh... so please don't depend on this too much.

> ### Environmental Tip of the Week
>
> The livestock industry accounts for 18% of the world's greenhouse gas emissions - more than all vehicular emissions combined. And beef production releases three times more greenhouse gases than chicken or fish. So, all else being equal, steer away from the burgers and opt for chicken.

Thanks for all of the feedback folks.

Dare to dream!
Scott

****

Err on the side of overcommunication, September 16, 2008

Dear Friends,

I hope everyone had a great weekend with their families and friends. I have learned over the course of my 17 years in Asia how important this holiday is. And, in our business that consumes many nights, weekends and days away, getting together with family at such holidays should be your first priority.

The Past Week

I have always been a person who believes in overcommunication. If you check and recheck things, rarely will you suffer from mixed or missed messages. Recently a client shared some comments with me about an event that took place in Beijing and Shanghai. They said many good things but also highlighted some key points for us to improve upon. We are blessed to have this type of feedback from our clients. Their main point is about getting every little detail right. They also show how clients compare us "office-to-office." I believe if we walked through these events with greater detail, we can prevent such things. The message here: err on the side of overcommunication.

Monday Morning Mail

> **Environmental Tip of the Week**
>
> Try to avoid ever using more than 1.5 line spacing in your word documents. First of all, 2-point line spacing looks a bit goofy. But more importantly, if we can reduce the lengths of our documents by 25%, when they are inevitably printed out we will save thousands of trees each year!

****

New Year's resolutions, December 29, 2008

Dear Colleagues,

As 2008 comes to an end, I want to begin this issue of the *Monday Morning Mail* by thanking you for indulging me throughout this past year. The *Monday Morning Mail* began from a recommendation by an employee for a need for more internal communication from the management team. It evolved into a sharing of cases, resources, a focus on digital and tips on how we can save the earth by taking small steps towards protecting our environment. I have enjoyed leading this, love the feedback I have received from all of you (good and bad) and promise to continue this in 2009. So, first and foremost, thank you.

As I look back on 2008 there is really so much to be thankful for. I continue to be amazed by how much we have accomplished, the quality of our client list, the strength of our team and the talent we have attracted. Many people say we have been very lucky, and I certainly believe that to be true. But I also believe people can create their own luck. And I, in part, credit all of us for nurturing this luck and creating our future.

So in the spirit of charting our future, I encourage all of us to take time to think through a few New Year's resolutions for 2009. I am told making resolutions during the New Year is universal. In my experience, a list of two to three you follow up and deliver upon is much better than five to 10. There are many people that talk about doing a lot of things and I think we should be the type of people who do less talking and more action. This is only my recommendation, but if we want to achieve great things most will need plans to do so and beginning with a New Year's resolution is a great place to start.

> **Environmental Tip of the Week**
>
> When you are out shopping this week (as most do during this time of the year), take a pass on the shopping bag and consolidate your things into one. Every little bit helps.

****

'Belief' and 'hope' in the future, January 23, 2009

Dear Friends,

As you prepare for the exciting Year of the Ox please take the time you normally spend reading the *Monday Morning Mail* (as I know everyone studies this intensely), and spend this with your family and friends and those most dear to you.

Take time to reflect on the past and prepare for the future. I am in the United States at the moment and just witnessed Obama's inauguration. There is "belief" and "hope" here that the future will be better than the past.

Let's together make the future happen for Ogilvy PR and thank you for all you have done.

****

Circles of influence, February 16, 2009

Dear Friends,

Have you ever thought about your "circle of influence"? I only ask you this because this topic came up several times this past week in meetings I was part of in the United States.

We are part of the largest and what I would hope most influential public relations firm in China. So in that context, I hope we all think about the networks that we create among journalists, analysts, business people, celebrities, professors, neighbors - anyone who wields some influence - and think about how these people help us learn more and do better work for our clients. I believe it is also a good exercise to think about what you stand for. What is the brand you have created for yourself? What is your point of view and how do you express this? As a PR person who should understand marketing and "influence", what do you do to get this across? Do you "punch above your weight?" All good questions to think about as you develop your career in public relations.

Chris Graves, Debby Cheung and I had a wonderful week in LA attending the Global Ogilvy PR Management Committee meeting. You would be proud of Ogilvy PR and the people that make up this group. Everyone is very smart, cordial, and wants to do everything possible to make the network work. They are proud of the Ogilvy China team and need us to be even more collaborative in the future.

Environmental Tip of the Week

In San Francisco this week I observed a lot about environmental actions the city is taking. In my hotel room there is a note that explains how much more energy it takes to clean the room of a "smoker" compared to a "non smoker." And, everywhere retailers ask if you "need a bag" and encourage you to shop with a recyclable bag. One thing we can all do is make sure we never need a paper bag with whatever we purchase. It is easily solved by bringing your own bag to whatever store you go to.

****

People

Steer clear of paper warfare, July 6, 2009

Dear Friends,

There has been a lot on my mind over the past two weeks. The purpose of the *Monday Morning Mail* is to share cases to learn from, resources that come my way, new ways that digital communications are entering our lives and thoughts on what we should be thinking about in terms of our own environment practices. Of course, I take the opportunity to lead this communication with my own message, and view of things as I see them from a client, staff and an organizational perspective. For those that read this often, thank you and I hope it is adding broader perspective to your career growth at Ogilvy. For those that don't, I worry you are missing good resources in all of the attachments. You can feel free to skip over my message, but there is a treasure trove of good presentations and information that you should have access to. I also want to apologize to our Hong Kong and Guangzhou colleagues, who often don't get much mention here. I am trying to get my arms around everything that is happening at Ogilvy PR in this region and am still learning to do so.

As we enter the depth of the summer, I continue to be optimistic about our prospects this year. We have huge pressure over the next six months to deliver what is now a stretch target, but I believe we can do so. There is a strong flow of new opportunities and many of our large clients have begun to spend. I also feel the market has picked up, and I just hope this momentum continues. The first half of this year makes me worry, though, about our own comfort level and new business skills. At Ogilvy, we are blessed with a continuing flow of opportunities. We are not as great "hunters" as we are "responders to briefs." But what happens when opportunity dries up? Where do you turn? What do we do to create new opportunities in the absence of someone knocking on the door? I think these are all questions for us to think about. What is the one opportunity you have brought to a client, or approached a new client with, when they did not expect this? I would love to hear your stories of "proactive business building" in the coming months so that we can refine our skills for the next wintery season.

There are two other things that I hope we all can consider. The first relates to our own communication with each other. David Ogilvy once commented, "I abhor people who wage paper-warfare". What I have found in a number of personal mistakes I have made is that emails do not smile. They don't often capture the true nature of what someone is trying to communicate. Emails have no personality. Yet, we have people who sit next to each other who use MSN, send emails and wage paper warfare. Do yourself a favor and sit down to have a conversation. Before sending a negative email, or message, work to try to understand the other person's view so that you don't make this mistake. I am as guilty as anyone here, but this company has been built on trust, partnership and respect, and these are all qualities we must work to maintain in good times and bad.

The second item is about value... once again. What value are we delivering day-in and day-out and how is this perceived. Chris Graves was in Beijing last week to spend two days training the leadership of Intel. Huge value that will deliver great returns for us moving forward. We got a brief from a Public Affairs client to ask what our fees would be to help save them millions of dollars in tariffs. If we succeed, what is the value of our service? We lost a pitch last week because the client did not feel we put enough emphasis on "measurement." There is a saying, "what gets measured, gets managed" and we must frequently check what is the value of the service we are providing and how is this being measured.

Environmental Tip of the Week

Stop reading this right now and check your monitor's brightness. If you can, lower it a notch or two. This will not only save energy but could be a little easier on your eyes. How much energy would you actually save? Basically, by doing this you could cut down on about 10 watts depending on your monitor.

So here is a little lunch-napkin math (somebody please check this!!!). If you do this for an hour you will save 0.01kWh. That doesn't sound like a lot, but Ogilvy PR has roughly 400 computer monitors running in China. So, if everyone made this change, we would save 4kWh of energy. If we all did this for a day, we would save 32kWh. If we all did this for a month we would save 640kWh. If we did this for a year we would save 7,680kWh. Or, if each kWh of electricity costs about RMB0.5, that's about RMB3,300 per year! Small changes can make a difference.

****

People

China in the spotlight, December 14, 2009

Good Day Friends,

As we enter this holiday season I would like to wish you and your family the very best. It has been an interesting year to say the least. Perhaps one of the most historic in my lifetime; and certainly for me living in China for the past 15 years and watching China truly emerge on the world stage. If we take a macro view, it feels like the center of influence in this world has changed. China is in the spotlight and how this story gets told will be most fascinating. The question I believe for all of us is what role do we plan to play in this story. We could be part of this, or watching it from the sidelines. And as the largest public relations firm with a very healthy client list I feel we have a real opportunity. Putting the China story aside, the Ogilvy PR story and your role in this has yet to be written. How will it play out? That is really for you and me to decide.

****

The link between discipline, desire and success, July 19, 2010

Dear Friends,

There's nothing like a short break with family and friends to refresh yourself. I encourage everyone to make sure you take time off as you not only owe this to those people in your life who put up with our crazy hours, but also to your clients and colleagues to ensure you have new experiences that will help you look at things and situations in a different way.

My one message this week continues on the theme of "discipline" and asks "what are you willing to do to become successful?" I am a person that believes that anything is attainable if you put your mind to it. You can master a new language, write a book, win a sporting competition, read 1,000 books - whatever it is. If you have the goal in mind and you are disciplined in achieving this, I believe it is possible. I was reminded of this in Shanghai this week. I arrived to the office at 9am after a breakfast meeting with a client. Getting into the elevator I was approached by two young ladies with notebooks. In broken English they begged to interview me for their university. I was in a rush, but I asked them to email me and I would find a chance for them to interview one of our staff in Shanghai. They wanted to know about our work in communications and needed 15 minutes to have a conversation. They emailed me, thanked me and told me they had been successful. That

Monday Morning Mail

after getting kicked out of the Center many times, this is where our office is, hiding in corners, finding anyway to speak with someone from Ogilvy, they finally succeeded and they were elated. Whoever spoke to them in Shanghai thank you. But this reminded me of a small lesson about discipline and desire and an unwavering commitment to success.

On the topic of discipline, I would like to remind everyone to be mindful of two things: One is the discipline of showing up to meetings and appointments "ON TIME!"; the second is how you dress. On the first topic, tardiness, in my view, is selfish, inconsiderate and unprofessional. If a meeting begins at 9:00am, please be sure you arrive at 8:59am. If you have a client appointment at 2:00pm, arrive five minutes early. If a deadline asks for you to deliver something by xxx, deliver it; and if for some reason you cannot, give the client adequate notice. While I know people love the freedom and openness of Ogilvy, this can only continue if we have self-discipline in making sure we get the basics right. The second topic about dress has been discussed many times. Even on casual Friday's, gym shorts are not permitted! Not even in the adidas or Sports Team. Flip-flops also. We need to look the part and many of you do not, and we need better discipline in how we look at this company. I am hoping that all of the directors and office leaders help me to enforce this.

At the moment I am getting caught up on happenings in all of the Greater China markets, and I want to thank everyone for the strong year we are having. We have an ambitious six months ahead of us and I am confident that if we get the discipline thing right we can be even more successful.

****

People

Are you ready to carry a heavy load? August 16, 2010

I personally believe everyone in this company should have to prepare and write an award case study. It is difficult to do this well and it is at the center of what we do. You will hear more about this soon, but we are going to use this as part of the key measurement criteria for people who rise at this company. Please do read through the cases that appear in this mail and others in the network and determine for yourself what makes great PR.

Did you read the travails of the CEO of HP last week? Have you studied the public relations ramifications of the CNOOC (China National Offshore Oil Corporation) spill? Never before have I been so excited that we are in the right business in the right place in the world. Clients are shifting budgets to us, the CEO offices are depending in greater ways on public relations, and huge deals are dependant on the positioning of such in Asia and world markets. And we are the people being asked how to position such things given global and local public sentiment. That's a heavy load. Are you ready?

****

Stepping back and taking stock, September 13, 2010

Dear Friends,

Well, I am feeling pretty good this morning. I had an absolutely great Friday and weekend. For those of you that were in Beijing on Friday, thank you for celebrating my 48th birthday. The cake was wonderful and the scarf from our H-Line colleagues was most appreciated. There are certain moments in one's life that we should step back and take stock of what we have. All of my bosses, Chris, Steve, TB, Shenan often talk about great organizations having great teams. And I certainly feel that way about Ogilvy PR. Our client list, the longevity of our people, the lack of real politics in a large organization, makes me really very proud. So thank you. I still feel that our work is only half done and that is really where I get my energy from.

****

Monday Morning Mail

Plan, network, succeed, November 22, 2010

Good morning friends,

There are three messages for this *Monday Morning Mail* that are on the top of my mind today.

First, the importance of plans and planning; second, the urgency to build out your networks; and third, the will to succeed.

The Importance of Plans and Planning

On Thursday of last week I was moved by a note I received from Liza Levy in our Shanghai office. She wrote, "Scott, when clearing up my things I found a note that I had written to myself at the PR Summit last year. It was a quick sketch of a year-long plan that I jotted down after you mentioned in your speech the importance of setting goals for yourself. In it included getting in to INSEAD (Institut Européen d'Administration des Affaires - the renowned Fontainebleau-based European Institute of Business Administration). It was then that I started the application process so would like to thank you so much! I had forgotten that was the beginning of it all. Thanks." Liza leaves us this week for INSEAD and while she will be missed, we should celebrate the fact that her plans are bearing fruit. Do you have a plan for yourself? I certainly hope Ogilvy PR figures into this but, most importantly, you need to be happy and feel you are progressing in life. There is nothing more liberating than understanding where you want to go, and I would love to help you get there.

The Urgency To Build Out Your Networks

I am increasingly convinced that the people in our organization that have broad networks and work to cultivate them are introduced to greater opportunities, clients, people and ideas. Our own Tom Crampton is a great testament to this. Joe Zhou in our Beijing office is also brilliant at this. The iPR team in Hong Kong and Ogilvy Financial team in Beijing exist off of referrals from their networks. You cannot build these networks sitting at your desks, eating lunch by yourself, staying at work until all hours and going straight home at night. In the spirit of planning, do you have your own plan to broaden your network and experiences? If you don't, I would hope you would consider this. Feel free to ask me about my own. :-)

The Will To Succeed

Those who know me well know that I respect tremendously people who push themselves to succeed. Success comes with a price and it is often painful,

People

but trust me that such prizes are more rewarding than a paycheck will ever be. We have a few people of late who have suffered the pain and pressure of client campaigns coming to their fruition. And for those of you feeling this ... just when you want to quit, I urge you to dig deeper. Your short-term pain will become your long-term gain. So if you are feeling the pain of the hard work, exhaustion and frustration, embrace this, see it through and check in with me in three months' time. These things have a way of paying dividends.

****

Monday Morning Mail

Have a personal plan, make it a reality, January 4, 2011

Dear Friends,

As the first *Monday Morning Mail* of 2011, I would like to begin with this message:

Please take care of you first in 2011!

Do you have a personal plan, and what are you going to do to make this a reality? I have a personal belief that if you are happy in your life, you will be a better professional and person because of this.

For me, I have three goals. First, I hope to write more regularly about what I am learning/have learned about doing business in China. Stay tuned. Second, I would like to make real progress in my language skills. I am embarrassed to have lived in China for so long and yet I cannot read nor write Chinese. Stay tuned. Third, I hope to finally get down to the weight I was when I graduated from college. Stay tuned. Too much? Perhaps. But I am putting in place some measures to track. I am 90kg, by the way, and hope to get to at least 86kg by year end. I am hiring a Chinese teacher to tutor me on weekends, and for the writing ... time will tell. What about you? Here is help if you haven't thought this through: the resolution tracker shared by Tim Isaac is absolutely brilliant.

Of course I have family goals as well that take precedence, but these are more personal in nature. And I have many Ogilvy PR-related goals that involve all of you.

Environmental Tip of the Week

I am delighted to report that the China International Public Relations Association released its 2010 TOP 10 China PR green company list and Ogilvy PR is the only international company on the list.

****

Do you have the heart for this business? November 21, 2011

Dear All,

Do you have the "heart" for this business?

This is the question I would like you to think about in this week's *Monday Morning Mail*.

On Thursday, Friday and Saturday of this past week I spent the afternoon of each day at the US-China Forum on Arts and Culture. A combination of Colleen's team and the Hero team supported this event and I am really most grateful to everyone who helped. In my experience working in China, this was one of the best conferences on soft power I have attended, and I was delighted we were part of this. In a press conference with Yo Yo Ma, Amy Tan, Joel Coen (a famous director) and others, Orville Schell of the Asia Society thanked Ogilvy many times. This conference is what Meryl Streep was in Beijing for and the news was everywhere. As a creative company, these are the events we like to be associated with, and I am most grateful to all who helped wave the Ogilvy flag here.

The reason I ask the question above is because by attending the conference and getting out from my regular environment - which I believe we absolutely MUST DO - I was working well into the wee hours of each evening last week. This was the cost of being out of the office and it was well worth it! Sometimes the choices we make impact other events that take time commitments and more that cause short-term pain. But in this case, the pain was well worth the investment. And in my view that takes heart. I associate this with taking time out for training, outside meetings or speeches that teach us new things. To be good and free we need to get outside of the office and into new environments. But that has a cost, as we also have commitments to work, our teams and other associated tasks. And these will often take you into the wee hours of the night. If you love what you do, this is not a problem at all. It is something that comes with the territory. If you aren't really into the business, well, such events create other frustrations that mount up and work adversely. If you are up at 1:00am working on a document and enjoying it because you made time for something else during the day, you are in the right place. If you hate this and everything about it, you need to think whether this is the right business. I realize this sounds a bit crazy, but I believe this. I loved last week and I was very tired at the end of the week. But I learned a ton. I have so many ideas as a result of this and feel refreshed. If you are not getting out from behind your desk and into the community, you need to do so. There is no manager at this company who will keep you from doing so as long as you communicate your ambition and what you are going to do to cover for this.

Monday Morning Mail

Make it happen, January 9, 2012

Close your eyes and picture this: "You are going on a vacation to a beautiful island, with nice beaches, rich in history, wonderful restaurants and great shopping. The forecasts say it is cloudy. You arrive and the sun is shining. The elements seem perfect. Your first day begins with a tasty breakfast and you have a week of sun, fun, shopping and dining ahead of you. And then... (write the end of this story for yourself).

Well, that is how I am feeling right now. We closed 2011 strong. My thanks to everyone who contributed to this. And we are starting the year in a good place. Strong relationships. Relatively happy people (I certainly hope). Endless opportunity ahead of us. Many people are prognosticating increased difficulties in 2012, but I remain optimistic. We have a strong North Asia team and I have full confidence in our abilities to take market share in any type of business climate. In reflecting on 2011 the one thing I am most proud of is the diversity of the people in our team. Someone once told me that Ogilvy is a place that attracts and tolerates all types of people. In my view, it is the right mixture of different types of people that can make us very powerful. I think it is the responsibility of all of us to understand that each and every person in this company has a place and role and we just must find exactly what that is and get the mix right.

If I was to write the end of the vacation story above, it would certainly be optimistic, rosy and exciting, filled with meeting interesting people, doing a lot of fun stuff with many pleasant surprises along the way. And while spontaneity would be a big part of this, it would be guided by decisions I would make that put us in the line of such experiences. And that is what I hope for all of us in 2012: for a year of excitement, success and opportunity. But this won't come without US making it happen. The message: we need to make such opportunities and experiences happen for ourselves. It is up to us and no one else!

Naturally, I am anxious for the year to come. My anxiety lies in a fear of complacency. We have many clients whereby our scope of work is entitled, "routine work". And I can tell you that "routine work" will not make people excited. We need great campaigns in 2012 that get people talking about how creative, smart and effective we are, and I hope we all talk more about the work product we create. I want us to win awards, not because of some fantastic write-up, but because the work is so great that it is a natural winner. And, I hope we can all be more disciplined in everything we do. Ogilvy PR in North Asia needs to be the place to work for the people who are serious about making public relations their career choice. The place where those passionate about public relations can make a living, innovate, learn, do cool stuff and have a lot of fun. This is my message for this *Monday Morning Mail* and where my mind is now.

So I am optimistic and anxious. And, I am sorry to say, I am still fat. I met 75% of my personal goals for 2011, but I am not the 87 kg, or whatever it was I committed to you in a previous mail. And I have lived with the fear of having to tell you this. I still have 5 kgs to go and I am committed to doing so in 2012. My problem is food ... sweets mostly. Chips too. And ice cream. And cheese. And French fries. And cheese fries. I can go on. :-) Whatever tastes good. Usually the rule in my family is that if I like it, it is not healthy. I need to address that and I am sorry to have to write this. So in 2012 I am committing to 87 kgs, to be confirmed by two witnesses, or I will give everyone who is a full time Ogilvy PR staffer in North Asia US$100 each. Enough about me.

We have two weeks before Chinese New Year and I know our colleagues in Korea and Japan also celebrate holidays this month. We need to make sure we put ourselves in opportunity's way in 2012. I am excited to be holding the planning summit in Beijing just out of the gates this year. I was delighted to hear about all of the new business wins as we closed 2011, particularly the GE win in Taiwan. We have the wind at our backs, and we need to use our unfair advantage to take market share.

****

Insecure overachievers, client impact and freestyle career pathing, February 6, 2012

Dear Colleagues,

During the holidays I had a chance to connect with a friend in Taiwan. This guy has worked at McKinsey for about a year and I was trying to understand a bit about their culture. He told me three things that I thought were quite profound that I would like to share with you.

The first thing he said was that people who succeed at McKinsey and the type of employees they try to hire are "insecure overachievers". These are people who are always anxious they are missing something, they are people who thrive on delighting clients and they will obsess and go to great lengths to be smart and stand out. This is exactly what David Ogilvy meant about "Divine Discontent". While I don't wish any of us to have any more insecurities than we do, this is something we should consider when hiring new people.

Monday Morning Mail

The second comment he made was that the whole culture of McKinsey is focused on one thing and one thing only: "client impact." Will their recommendation have an impact on the client's organization? Seems to me that this is taking a page from our "creativity and effectiveness" drive. I urge us to think about what impact our work is having on our client's organization and what we are doing about that.

Finally, when he was speaking about himself, he said that staff at McKinsey were recommended to "find their own McKinsey". What he means is that new opportunities, jobs, expertise areas, and more are not prescribed. They need to be teased out and discovered by the employees. Career tracking is as much the responsibility of the staffer as it is the organization. I feel very much the same way about Ogilvy. There are so many opportunities in this company. If you build an expertise, make a case for it, you can do it. It is "freestyle career pathing". Find what interests you, make sure it fits into Ogilvy's overall business strategy, build an expertise that is valued by clients and go do it. Who knows, you could be the next Entertainment, Sports, Financial or Impact practice. My advice in North Asia... create your own Ogilvy!

We have started the year in all markets with renewal of contracts and campaigns and a lot of new business. I have had conversations with many directors about the fear of complacency. We have many clients that are doing just great, they love us and many appreciate us. But they ask at this time of the year, what am I missing? Can someone else provide a new perspective? I would like us to instill some sort of discipline that has us going to clients unsolicited to say ... "we have been at this campaign for a year now, we are coming in to share with you the next phase of this. We have brainstormed and this is what is next." I also think this needs to be steeped in research. I fear that, with the pace of things today, taking time out to dig deep into the market and the audience groups we are communicating with is being diminished. Great insights need rigor and that is what I hope we can bring into our practices in 2012.

Insights. Impact. Divine Discontent. Proactivity. Finding Your Own Ogilvy. Seems to me a good way to start the Year of the Dragon.

IMPORTANT: We have sponsored a major study on "Crisis in the Weibo (Microblogging) Era" that is due out in February. We are going to make a lot of noise with this so please involve clients, media and others as we kick this off next week. Debby Cheung is leading this effort and you will see more on this soon.

****

The glass half full, February 20, 2012

Dear Colleagues, Friends,

Do you have belief? I am not asking about religious belief here, I am writing about belief that your dreams can come true. That sometimes the impossible is really possible. Well, look no further than what is happening in the US with Jeremy Lin, the new Chinese American, who has taken the world by storm at the New York Knicks. This Harvard-educated guy is full of personality, fun to watch and a role model for all. The most inspiring thing, though, is his continued pursuit of his dream. He was not recruited heavily out of high school, did not get drafted out of college, slept on friends' couches, and today within a two-week span, he has reached the likes of the very best in terms of fame in the National Basketball Association (NBA).

I am reminded of this as I tour around North Asia and listen to all of your wishes, hopes, dreams and concerns. We have entered the year in a strong position, but some of us have big new business gaps, client issues, team challenges and personal concerns you are dealing with. My advice here, and the way I deal with these things, is to look at every situation as a learning exercise; an experience you are faced with that will help you grow in one way or another. It's looking at the glass "half full" instead of "half empty". A friend once told me that every day he is above ground is a good day. :-) That is a bit extreme, but most of us live lives that the majority of people in the world would dream of. Take stock of your situation and what role you play in this world, look at the positive side and develop a plan for making it happen. You will certainly improve the odds in helping your dreams come true.

We should not forget that creating and executing high-impact communications campaigns, and providing strategic communications counsel, is what we are about. And in doing this we will attract the very best in the industry, we will win new clients and our existing clients will give us opportunities to do more. That was my message in the Webex that took place this past week.

****

Monday Morning Mail

Figuring out what matters to you, September 3, 2012

Dear Friends,

What matters to you? I hope you can take some time to think about this in the coming months as I personally believe the things that you really care about you will do something about. I would imagine that your family, friends and your health are at the top of the list. But what is that one thing at work - at Ogilvy - that you really care about?

I got to thinking about this last week. There was a speaker that came into Beijing to talk about a topic that I was interested in. The topic was "Cultural IQ" and he spoke about learning to understand cultural differences. There were a number of meetings I was asked to attend on this day, but since I rarely have the chance to attend the trainings at Ogilvy I insisted that I get outside of the office and attend this speech. I went and I learned a ton. I am writing about this because I am so happy that I made it a priority to attend this. In life and work there are always going to be things pulling you here and there. A large percentage of the time you are going to be attending meetings that don't do anything for you, but you are obligated to join because your boss or your client asks you to. Regardless of their content, these meetings are important and it goes with the work we are in. But I encourage you to think hard about what you really care about ... what matters to you professionally ... and to seek out a path on your own to improve yourself. At Ogilvy we are going to dish up a ton of opportunities for you to learn, but a large part of the responsibility for your own education, particularly on what matters to you most, must be taken on by you.

****

Pace yourself for a marathon, not a sprint, May 20, 2013

We have had better weeks.

By now you have heard from us a few times on the tragic loss of Gabriel Li in Beijing. You have probably seen it discussed in the online community and read about it in the newspapers. Some of the coverage has been accurate of the events that happened as we know them. Other coverage has been erroneous. Much of the online discussion has been emotional. What we learned in Chris Graves' visit to Beijing and his subsequent training on storytelling is that in such circumstances no one cares about facts. And in such a sad series of events, why care about the facts? Gabriel is gone. He was a great guy. He was 24 years old (25 this Sunday) and he was a big brother figure despite his age. He was true Ogilvy and what I learned about him this past week makes me feel even worse because I wish I had got to know him better.

What Gabriel's passing must signify is that we all must take care of our health. Eat better. Exercise. Pace yourself. Find ways to relieve our stress. Most importantly we must look at how we spend our time and if we are working too much overtime we need to take action. Please let me know first. The next step for us in this event is to look at what more we must do to make our office, environment and profession more healthy.

I must tell you that I am more resolved than ever to the business of public relations. I went into this business nearly 30 years ago because I saw the power of the public relations professional in being the purveyor of the truth and honesty in working with journalists representing companies to help them tell the truth. Today the world has changed dramatically. I worry a lot about the changing face of global media and where people are going to get well-researched unfiltered truth about a particular story. In Gabriel's case a simple tweet made it into a local newspaper and media outlets globally ran the story from this newspaper without checking any details. My daughter, on hearing me talk about Gabriel's case at home and the way the global media was covering it, said to me: "Dad, get with it. Nobody believes the news today." This incident alone shows how important and relevant our role is in today's world and what is to come.

It was a long and deeply meaningful week. Take care of your health please. Like me, I hope your career at Ogilvy is more of a marathon than a sprint and we need you to pace yourself.

****

Monday Morning Mail

Find a way to be generous, July 1, 2013

Last week, on Monday June 24, my father passed away. What has been most poignant about the whole experience of losing him has been the importance of memories. Everyday we create memories for ourselves, some more lasting than others. In my experience, the memories that are most meaningful come from interactions with other people. They don't come from sitting behind a desk immersed in your own world. And for me, fortunately, my mind stores the positive memories and has somehow discarded the negative.

At my dad's funeral service his colleagues, many of whom worked with him for more than 40 years, came over to talk about their own memories of working with him. His work was a big part of his life and he had a rich life evidenced by all of the wonderful comments that were shared with me.

Before he died my dad told me his wish was to do something to improve one person's life everyday. It is similar to a comment Charlotte Beers, one of our past CEOs, once shared as the secret to success in our careers. Her comment was simple, "be generous." Be generous with your time, in helping others, with our clients. With your family.

So that is my simple message for this *Monday Morning Mail*. Find a way to be generous ... and the crazy thing is that your own life will be better because of this.

As a call-out for this *Monday Morning Mail*: the entire Ogilvy PR North Asia Network. Thank you for what you have done and for all of the memories you have provided me with over the years.

****

Learn from Steve Dahloff, December 9, 2013

A *Monday Morning Mail* salute to Steve Dahllof!

"FIND YOUR OWN OGILVY!" In Steve's remarks last Wednesday he said the greatest thing about his career is that no one ever told him what he was going to do. He created the path. We didn't have a Strategy & Planning unit... he set it up. We didn't have a creative unit in Washington, he set it up. He saw Social in Asia as a possibility to leap our business forward, and he put $$ behind this and fully supported Thomas Crampton's plans for Social in Asia. You see Steve was not working for the day he retired, he was enjoying the journey all along by experimenting here and there and creating opportunities for himself. When I think about all of the opportunities and challenges ahead of us, I can come up with about 10 other jobs that don't exist that would make sense. So if there is anything we can learn from Captain Dahllof it is to not let someone else define how you are going to live your life at this company. Look at everything we have around us and begin to chip away a path that is unique to you. Success in this business does not come from showing up and working towards retirement. It comes from a job brief that is so exciting that you cannot wait to arrive at the office to tackle it. And, by the way, decent money comes along with that. It stops being the reason you work, and it serves as a result of something that is truly valuable to yourself and the company. I will send another mail in due course about the life and times of Steve Dahllof, but let's learn from Steve on this one. Perhaps you too can turn 60 and look like you are 50 while doing so.

****

Always make time for training, May 12, 2014

This *Monday Morning Mail* is prepared for anyone at Ogilvy PR that manages another person and is written in support of all of the young people who work at our firm. The beginning is written from the perspective of a young person.

"Dear Ogilvy PR Supervisor,

Thank you for choosing me to work at Ogilvy PR. This company is great and it is really a lot of fun. I can't believe work can be so much fun. There is also so much to learn here so thank you for giving me the opportunity. The hours are crazy but I really don't mind as I am learning every day. The pay could be better :-), but I understand I have to prove myself first. The people here are really very special and I feel I can learn from them. So thank you.

I am writing, however, to ask you for one favor. Let me know that you are thinking about my future! Here's why: Everyone knows that shit rolls downhill. And when our workload is really crazy, it's like we are swimming in a sewer. I don't mind getting coffee and doing whatever to service the client and the team, but I want to grow professionally at this company. The one thing that I value is my freedom, but I understand work takes precedence and that will cut into my plans most of the time. But, and this is a big BUT, please allow me to attend speeches, training and activities that will help me develop myself professionally. I will work nights and weekends, but I really get upset when I have been invited to professional development activities and I am told I cannot attend because something urgent has come up from the client. What I have learned, dear supervisor, is that urgent things for

Monday Morning Mail

the client happen everyday and every hour. That is the norm in this business. Do you think we could have a system at our company that plans for such contingencies? The greatest benefit of this company for us is what we can learn and I really hate missing training. So that is my ask. I want to know that you are looking out for me. I want to be like you someday, and if I am, I promise the one thing I will do is shoulder some of the urgent client work so that my team members can develop their skills. Thank you for taking the time to read this."

This was written by me, but it reflects many conversations I have had with young people at Ogilvy PR. We spend fortunes on training and time at this company and we need to cultivate a learning culture. We need to give our people room to learn. In return the gift you will get is a team member that grows in competence and stays with you along the way.

****

Organization

Love the matrix and the matrix will serve you. If we knew how much we knew we would be dangerous.

Chapter Three

Organization

Focus on the fundamentals, October 20, 2008

Dear Friends,

Bravo Shanghai! I hope all of you were as proud as I was watching the Ogilvy PR Professional Achievement Awards last week and watching the Johnson & Johnson team walk away with the Corporate Award for the "Power of One" Internal campaign.

Here's a test: When someone asks you what you do, how do you reply? I think it is important that we gain some clarity around how we talk about our business. And there is no other way to crystalize this than to use the discipline of writing case studies to do this. I certainly hope the work we do day-to-day fits into a broader "award winning" campaign that achieves results for our clients. Great work that delivers results will be our best defense against difficult times and our standards must be even higher than our clients when it comes to the work we do.

Great agencies are built by committed people who have strong fundamentals; fundamentals such as writing, research, client service, follow up, discipline, speaking, creativity, teamwork. I remember reading an article about Michael Jordan, the great Chicago Bulls basketball player. In the article all he talked about was fundamentals: passing, shooting, dribbling, teamwork, and this was what made him such a great player. We are good... with moments of greatness. Mediocre belongs to other agencies. Let's focus on the fundamentals as we close the year and enter 2009 and this will surely carry us through.

****

Thoughts on strategy and execution, March 9, 2009

Dear Colleagues,

Strategy and Execution. These are two words you will hear repeatedly this year. What's the strategy? And how to execute? I sat in several client meetings this week that addressed these topics. In my training the strategy is the "decisions a company takes to achieve its goals or objectives." The execution is the actual "how to make it happen." I once attended a wonderful Ogilvy training (note to those people who seem to skip these), who invited a management guru to speak to us about strategy and execution, and the intersection of these concepts. His comment, "strategy is what you do as a company." Now there are a lot of companies who talk a lot about what they aspire to. But their aspirations are far from what they really do as a company. And in my opinion, what you really do as a company is where you should begin to build from. We may want to be great communications strategists (and we should aspire to be), but what our clients want is for us to manage their media relationships. My point here is that we need to be grounded in what we do well (for example, messaging and connecting clients with the strategic media to convey this messaging), and aspirational in our practice. This was the theme of this week for me as I spoke to many people about what they really do and I found it hard for them to be gut-level honest about this. Some people would say, I am a "marketing strategist." But what they do is creative for promotions. Again, we must have the broad vision in place, but we also need to know what we really do. That is my view, at least, and it is open for debate. These times both strategy and execution are very important and we need to be clear that clients want us to do both.

Environmental Tip of the Week

Now that Spring is here, go out and get a bicycle if you don't have one already. Not only is it great exercise and cost-effective, but it makes a strong contribution to improving our local environment (and traffic!).

****

Monday Morning Mail

Letter from Nepal, August 30, 2010

I begin this week's *Monday Morning Mail* sitting in the hotel lobby in Kathmandu, Nepal preparing to head back to Beijing. My inbox is full with reports from staff who have been called in for crisis help related to the air crash last week in Yichun. Thank you both for diving in and leading this effort. At the same time, the Nokia team has launched Nokia's newest mobile phone, the N8, with a microblog press conference. The attention has been huge and there have been issues around this as well that the team has been managing. And, while all this is going on, the search for the Pambassador Campaign in Chengdu has become viral. There is a buzz in the air and it can surely be felt.

For me this week has been a milestone in my career. I have lived in Asia for nearly 20 years and never once thought of coming to Nepal. Although the beauty of Mt. Everest is well known, I had no idea of the lively culture and opportunity this country has in the area of tourism. There is something here for everyone: temples, villages, festivals, museums, white water rafting, safaris, beginner trekking where you can see Everest. I have been here for five days with Tsinghua University and it is really not enough. I didn't have the chance to see the birthplace of the Lord Buddah... a place called Lumbini. If you have 10 days holiday and you want a raw, natural experience, you must come here.

The highlight of the trip, however, was meeting the President and sharing my views on how to brand Nepal.

I also spoke to the Young Entrepreneurs Association, and travelled through the country with Dean of the Tsinghua University Journalism School, Li Xiguang, and 10 students and faculty members. We sponsor the Dean's Freshman journalism program called, "Writing on the Road." The students are all very impressive and you would be proud we sponsor such a program.

We were also the guests of TVJ, an independent television station in Kathmandu and the reporters were all hugely accommodating. There is no better way to get to know a country than to be the guest of its #1 journalist organization and I am very much indebted to Dean Li and Tsinghua and to Ogilvy for giving me this opportunity. And what is even better is that I believe we are soon to get a brief for helping Nepal attract Chinese tourists and some of you will be given the same opportunity as I was.

****

Organization

Pitching in to help the Korean team, October 11, 2010

Dear Colleagues,

With this *Monday Morning Mail* I would like to welcome our Korean team to the distribution. I had the honor to visit our offices in Seoul on the first day of the October 1 holiday and had a most delightful visit. Not only did I get to spend time with the Managing Director there, Joyce Kim, but I also met some of the staff and learned about the work we are doing in Korea. I also did some work of my own. Thanks to the tenacity of Joyce, we have been appointed as the PR partner for the Korea Bid Committee for the World Cup in 2022 (KOBID). Joyce kindly put me on the Korean team, as much of the work is English copywriting. I had the chance to meet the Secretary General of KOBID, who is the main spokesperson and a most charismatic man. He was the former Ambassador for Korea to the UN and is a very well spoken gentleman. In becoming his copywriter I signed up for an all-nighter in the midst of the October Holiday, as the Secretary General prepared to face FIFA on October 6 after being given eight surprise questions 12 hours prior to their meeting in London. That meant that Joyce and I received these questions at midnight and the two of us worked through the evening to prep the team. The lesson here is that you are never too old to pull an all-nighter. This project is lots of fun and very rewarding and we will be fully involved in the next month as the Bid gets decided on December 2.

****

Client 'chemistry' and network 'curiosity', October 25, 2010

Dear North Asia Colleagues,

With this *Monday Morning Mail* we welcome our Ogilvy PR Japan colleagues to our community. I had a chance to visit this office on October 26th and 27th and learned very much about Japan, our offering and the importance of our network. So welcome Japan! The *Monday Morning Mail* is a twice-monthly note from me that aims to share news that's happening around our region, thoughts about our business and, most importantly, case studies and resources that pop into my email that may not make it to yours. The aim is to share and inform and to create a community amongst all of us in North Asia.

There are two messages I would like to share in today's note. The first centers around "chemistry" and the importance of getting this right in our client relationships. The second is around "curiosity" and taking advantage of what is in this network to improve ourselves professionally.

Monday Morning Mail

Chemistry

This is the theme of this week because I had no less than five meetings with clients last week who wanted to speak with me about this. The first meeting I had was very good and spoke about our strong support for Intel during the CEO's visit late last month. The conversations the rest of the day deteriorated from there. The clients I spoke with actually didn't care about how smart or creative we were, the messages were, "can you change the team", "find the right match", "give us someone fresh." Let me remind everyone of the words of David Maister that I think so highly of. He counsels, "clients don't care how much you know until they know how much you care." And these words seem more appropriate now than ever. We have always been a firm that is hugely client oriented so please make sure your clients know you love them. Be generous. Meet them often and come with surprises in ideas and how we can improve. Own their agendas. And please go the distance to understand key things that can help you get the chemistry right. We will not be able to grow and do the client work we need to do if you can't get chemistry right.

Curiosity

I sat in the "Multiple Personality" digital session on Friday in Beijing and there were only six people in attendance. In an office where we have some 250 people, that is awful. Now I am not angry that people don't attend every session offered, because there is a ton going on, but it makes me question what each of us are doing to improve ourselves. If it is not painfully clear, understanding digital and digital channels is where the industry is going... these are the areas where your clients' constituencies get their news and if you don't know this you will be a dinosaur soon. Since I am close to being the oldest person in our network I expect all of you younger people to understand digital. And Tom Crampton and his crew in Hong Kong are doing everything possible to get you up to speed. What are you doing to come to the table?

****

Organization

Respect is an absolute must in our business, April 25, 2011

Dear Colleagues,

I hope this *Monday Morning Mail* is finding you as optimistic as I am about our business. I am coming off of a very busy weekend that was spent with our CEO, Miles Young, at the Tsinghua 100th Year Anniversary. This was a premier networking event for us and I had the chance to meet many CEOs and people of influence in China. I also had wonderful seating at the remarks given by President Hu. After experiencing all I did this week, I certainly feel we are in the right channels of influence in this market.

I continue to feel good about our prospects. We are experiencing ongoing opportunities across all markets in North Asia and that is a good thing. Our business is certainly in growth mode. However, I do feel all is not perfect. We have spots where complacency sets in and this results in troubled client relationships. Or, we have clients experiencing their own challenges and we find it difficult to navigate these. I fear this client situation is more the norm now, and all of us are going to need maturity and experience in how to navigate client relationships who are experiencing their own internal challenges.

The other note of caution from me is to remind everyone that we must respect ourselves, our colleagues and our clients at all times. For me, respect is an absolute must in our business. We depend on each other too much and tolerating even a minor dose of disrespect can spoil an entire office. This week I have engaged in a few conversations related to respect, and I beg you all to work at "connecting" and ensuring your message is heard before screaming, yelling or accusing someone of something. We cannot force people to work for us. We need to encourage them to want to go far beyond what is expected to delight. With proper teaming and encouragement I am confident we will deliver results beyond the expectations of our clients.

****

Monday Morning Mail

The importance of marking milestones, July 4, 2011

Dear Friends:

Traditions. Defined by Webster's dictionary a tradition is "an inherited, established or customary pattern of thought, action or behavior." Traditions, in my view, are behaviors that ground us in the past that in many ways help to guide us into the future.

So, this weekend, on the very month we mark the 100th year of David Ogilvy's birth, we celebrated in China Ogilvy's founding 20 years ago. Marked by parties, tree plantings (to further strengthen our roots in China), a few speeches and more, the Ogilvy Group partied to mark our 20 years in China and the future possibilities that are yet to come. We also recognized the Ogilvy loyalists on this day with the traditional "Gold Coin" presentations. This is an Ogilvy China tradition, and something that has deeper meaning for many who reach anniversary milestones. I am very proud to say that more than 40% of the recipients in Beijing this year were from Ogilvy PR or H-Line Ogilvy. Nearly 25% of the staff receiving 10-year coins were from PR (the back office having the most recipients). In Beijing we had one 20-year recipient. That is yours truly for reaching 20 years of service in Greater China. I feel proud and grateful for all this company has done for me over the 20 years and I only hope that all of you have the same experiences and opportunities that I have been given. I read many facebook, weibo and blog-posts about different staffers' celebration of their coins and I would like to recognize all of the recipients.

Just after the Beijing ceremony someone came up to me and said, "I can't wait to get my 20-year coin." I responded, "I can't wait for this as well, and for you to receive your 30-year coin!" I certainly hope we continually improve our retention rates of those people who want to make public relations their career, and I promise to do whatever I can to make Ogilvy a place for people to work, learn and grow.

The gold coins are just one of the traditions that define the Ogilvy culture and one that I am so grateful that TB and Shenan created at the very beginning. One other tradition I favor is the "Welcome Lunch" for new staff members. I want to claim ownership of this one in China, although others may lay the same claim. When I first began working some 26 years ago, I was so excited to join a small PR firm in New York. I remember for lunch that day I had lunch by myself. I was so excited to join the workforce and yet lonely and left out by others who fended for themselves. I vowed that when we set up our offices in China we would develop a "welcome lunch" tradition and

Organization

invite new staffers out to lunch to celebrate the first day of the rest of their lives with us. Please, please all managers out there, continue this tradition. It is such a small thing to do that has such a lasting impression on the kind of people we are.

That's all for now on Ogilvy traditions. There are many more. As we grow, evolve, twist and turn, marking certain milestones is important in helping to remember who we are and where we have come from.

****

Securing investment and delivering more value, October 10, 2011

Dear Colleagues,

For Ogilvy PR, the period of late September and October is about planning for all of us in North Asia. Trying to read the tea leaves for the next year, make some bets, prioritize where we spend our time, think through what would be a BIG move, and consider where we should spend less time. If I asked any of you: "we have US$100,000 to spend on some sort of investment, what should we do?" What would you do? I would love to hear your thoughts! For the record, we are asked this all of the time and if we have some good ideas, I am certain we can get this money. Yet, I caution you, with investment we must also deliver a return. So just like you may make an investment in a stock, or real estate or something else, so must we promise a return on our investment. Just so you know, and contrary to popular belief, when we go into these budget sessions we always ask for investment for our people. "We need more money to pay our good people" is the common request. And I believe every senior manager at this company gets this. And while we ask for this, we must also consider with such an ask that our cost base rises. So the logic goes that with more cost, we must ensure our clients value us greater than ever before. And as they value us more, we need to ensure that they will allow us to charge more, bill more and do more work. This whole theme of "VALUE" is a never ending topic in our business, and the more we drill down on the key questions ... "what do clients value" ... "what do our people value" ... "how to continue to deliver more value" ... this will ultimately lead towards our growth.

On a side note, I certainly hope that along with our company plans each of you have your own personal plans on what you are working towards and trying to accomplish for yourselves. And the more your personal plans dovetail with your career plans, in my opinion, you will be led to continuous bliss. And wouldn't that be nice.

****

Food for thought, March 5, 2012

Dear Friends,

So let me share a bit on what I am focused on and what is worrying me. I will keep this to five points.

First, is the work we are doing truly making an impact? I feel we have had impact with IBM's Smarter Planet campaign, and with our work for Chengdu. The Madame Tussauds work is strong and I would imagine that is having an impact. But across the board are we making a dent? I hope you will ask yourselves that question every day.

Second, how committed are we to digital transformation? And how is this story going to develop? And what is our competitive edge? Make no mistake that we are fully committed to evolving our digital offerings and capabilities and everyone must embrace this.

Third, are we evaluating opportunities properly, and when we decide to pitch for new business, are we doing everything possible to win? I have a personal objective to help us all better manage the time we spend with clients, with our own development and in the pursuit of new opportunities.

Fourth, how proactive are we? I worry a lot that once we get briefed and get on with our work, or as we are conducting our campaign work, we forget that clients want continual new ideas, information, free thinking. We need to somehow inject a discipline of surprising our clients with new and different things that help them build their businesses.

Fifth, are we connecting? That means connecting with each other, leveraging the vast resources we have, connecting with our clients and connecting in the communities. How deep are we really into the fabric of what is happening in all of our markets and what must we do to have more influence on what happens?

Organization

This is just some food for thought as we enter a new week. I have great ambition for all of us and I hope you will join me in working to realize this ambition.

****

Don't hold back, don't wait for tomorrow, make it happen today,
March 19, 2012

Dear Friends,

How connected are you? Please give this question a few minutes of thought.

This weekend I spent at the China Development Forum (CDF) at the Diaoyutai State Guest House, one of the top Chinese Government meeting facilities, with Joe Zhou, our head of Public Affairs in China, Mac Brodie and about 1000+ CEOs, academics, government officials and more. For networking in China this is the #1 event to attend. Martin Sorrell, WPP CEO was there as were many, many others. I attended a dinner with Martin Sorrell on Friday night and he asked all of the WPP operating companies who would be attending the CDF. No response, only Ogilvy PR. Very proud.

But it made me think about our true strength as a company in the markets where we operate. How much are we an observer of what is happening vs. being part of shaping what is taking place? I would argue the PR firms who are shaping the environment are presented with much richer opportunities than those as observers. And those PR firms that are connected are in the lens of those big opportunities.

So how to make that happen for you? First, get out of the office. Connect with people who are doing different things. Have conversations. Have a target list of people doing interesting things and try to meet with them. Don't be shy! Don't ask, why would they like to meet with me? Use Ogilvy's brand to forge conversations that will take you into new areas. When I was young (years and years ago) I asked a few journalists out to lunch. I wondered, "why would they like to have lunch with me?" But I asked anyway. Many of those who accepted are my very close friends today.

Nothing is holding you back. Don't wait for tomorrow. Make it happen today.

****

Monday Morning Mail

Practice 'confident modesty' and never be arrogant, April 23, 2012

Dear Friends,

I write to you this Monday with mixed emotions. On one hand I feel very proud, confident and inspired. On the other I am concerned and anxious. Allow me to explain.

On the positive side, I am happy because our business is plugging along. We have a number of very lucrative new business assignments ahead of us, we are doing some very strong work with current clients and winning public recognition for this, and I truly believe we have the best people in the industry working at Ogilvy. I am inspired by many of the pictures shared by those staff who participated in the "Optimism For The Future Contest". These are truly uplifting. And I got a lot of optimism and inspiration this weekend from attending a birthday party for twin 80 year-olds. The messages these gentlemen and their wives shared about the secret recipe in life were most moving. They recommended to find a partner that you can trust 100% of the time and to live life in a truthful and honest way. They commented about surrounding yourself with happy, "can do" people as another ingredient to lifelong happiness. As I write this I am truly feeling optimistic and grateful for all that has come our way. I am thankful for working with all of you and our clients and I believe we have to just keep these simple but meaningful instructions in mind as we follow the paths of our lives.

On the concerned side, I have one very important message to send to everyone. The one message I have for you is that "arrogance" of any nature will not be tolerated at Ogilvy PR. I was reminded of this in a conversation with someone last week who told me that Ogilvy is so big and so plentiful with clients and opportunities that "you guys are untouchable," they commented. They said this both admiringly and alarmingly. They said you turn down opportunities if you are not interested, you insist clients adjust to your way of doing things instead of being flexible, and you have people of mixed ability that carry themselves with a false posture of confidence. And when there is a problem with you and the client, you always blame the client for not understanding. Most of all you cannot take criticism. Now this person is very close to me and so some of these comments were directed at me, but I see this as well in some of you and I just want to send out a cautionary note of concern that we should never, ever be arrogant in anything we do. Being proud and confident, committed to great campaigns and being the brains behind these are important. Closing your mind and ears to constructive criticism is not. I prefer that people see us as David Ogilvy wished: as an organization that operates with "Divine Discontent." A company who hires and nurtures "Gentlemen and Gentlewomen with Brains." I think we should practice "confident modesty" and I hope we can all embrace this. That is the big "concern" message today.

****

Reflect on people and relationships, May 7, 2012

Dear Friends,

My message to all of you today is to never forget that we are a company made up of people and relationships, and we are defined by the people we work, live and surround ourselves with. And during the course of your career there will be people who have differential influence on your careers and we should take time out to celebrate them and be thankful for all they have done.

By now you will have received a message from our Global Chairman, Shelly Lazarus, who announced her retirement as Chairman of the Ogilvy & Mather Group, to become Chairman Emeritus. Chairman Emeritus is a person who has retired from a position but retains a professional title and a relationship with the company and has some responsibilities that carry on. Many of you have had the opportunity to meet Shelly over the years. I feel very lucky to have known and worked for her and I think we all owe her a very big thank you for her leadership. Shelly has been with Ogilvy for 40 years. In a business where people jump from here and there, this type of commitment is unique. I know she has had influence on many great campaigns over the years. She is the person who placed Miles in Asia and then as the CEO in New York, and she is the key person who helped this company win and grow our largest global client over many years, IBM. To me she is a "Client Leader" - a person who truly loved her clients - and someone with a great ability to identify leadership in people and let them lead. The Ogilvy & Mather culture today has been fostered by her and we owe much of what we have today to her support of China. She was incredibly generous with her time and commitment to this company and I am grateful for all she has done.

Take a moment to think about the people and relationships you have created here and reflect on how these have shaped who you are today.

****

Monday Morning Mail

Great teams are what win championships, June 18, 2012

Dear Friends,

My message this week is about TEAMWORK and the importance of the roles we play in our various teams. Whether I was in the office reviewing client work, chatting with staff, or meeting with clients, this concept has occupied my mind this week. Even in my down time, watching the NBA Finals, or the Euro Cup, it is clear to me that great teams are what win championships, not individual performances. Shenan Chuang, Ogilvy Group CEO for China, once explained to me that she knows early on when she is going to have a good year. She told me that when the management team is really a team, no one can stop us. I have reflected on this as I evaluate our performance in each of the Ogilvy PR offices in North Asia. When the team is right, we are formidable. When it is not, you can recognize the difference. I have a personal belief that everyone on this earth has been put here to do one thing really well. There is no good and bad staff. It is incumbent on a manager to find the right mixture of people to create a winning team. And the good news is that even if you don't have the right "qi" now, it is reparable. We have had teams who were once down in the dumps in China that are thriving now. We have had teams that were high performance in one year, that are a bit off-kilter now. It is not life and death, but if you are not winning a disproportionate share of your opportunities it is time to consider what must be done. And that is my message today. Please think about your teams and the roles you play in your teams. How are you shaped up and how are you contributing to the collective result, beyond your individual performance? If you are out there and working by yourself and constantly frustrated by others' contribution, part of the problem could be you. If you have created something that is just not working as good as it was, the problem could have been created by you. The second message here is to please don't look to others to blame or change this. Be the change you want to see happen. This is a soft message with very big importance, I believe.

****

Organization

Recipe for great PR, July 1, 2012

I have a simple recipe to what makes a great PR firm and that is the right combination of good people, great client relationships and fantastic work. If we get this mixture right we will be unstoppable. So at this time of the year, I hope you are engaged in at least one very exciting campaign for your clients. If you are not, I suggest you speak to your supervisor and see what you must do to do something that is totally outside of the box and wows them. There is no better time for this than now!

****

Critically evaluate what you can and cannot do, July 16, 2012

Nearly a decade ago I attended a training by David Maister, the master of managing professional service firms, and author of many popular books. I was lucky to be part of this at the invitation of WPP. David Maister is a great trainer and shared one lesson that has stuck with me throughout, and that lesson is this: *"**strategy is what you do as a company.**"* What this means to me is that the summation of what you do... makes up a core part of your strategy. For example, in public affairs, we provide counselling, access and information about government audiences and we do this better in some industries than others. That is what we do. It is what we get paid for and what clients want. We can have ambition to build out other competencies in the future, but it is difficult to claim "experience" and "expertise" in areas we want to deliver, but never have done so. I always feel it is best to deeply understand what you do, and what clients pay for, improve that expertise and grow incrementally from there.

So when you are thinking about your business or your own expertise, please be highly critical of evaluating what you do and do well and hone that skill before dreaming about the next level. I have sat in too many meetings of businesses that "want" to do xyz with no experience. The success rate of these business leaders is very small. Rather, figure out what clients want, what you do and grow from there.

****

Creating a cycle of positive energy, September 24, 2012

Dear Friends,

The theme of today's *Monday Morning Mail* centers around THE WORK WE DO. I have a very simple way of looking at high-performance public relations firms and teams. The formula goes like this: Great PR teams deliver great work! Great work attracts great people. Great work makes people happy and feel like their work is making a difference. Great work retains star staff. It makes more money and changes a conversation on the client side from cost to value. Great work gives us more room to pay people more and do more things. It gives us a freedom to do more great work and creates a cycle of positive energy and contributes to high-performance cultures. So in the wake of Q3 reporting, of "final stretches to meet financial numbers", of 2013 budgets and of a focus on numbers, numbers, numbers, let's not forget that we are in the business of "ideas" and developing and executing ideas that build our clients' businesses. Please ask yourself if what you are doing is part of a "Great Work" effort. Are you proud of this and the results and are your clients proud to be associated with the work? If the answers to these questions are yes, wonderful. If not, think about what you must do to change that dynamic.

****

Embrace the belief that you are masters of your own destiny, December 10, 2012

So as we near the close of the year I would like to ask everyone for their best effort in closing 2012. We are in the last 2 miles of a 52-week marathon and we need a strong end. As you reflect on your own year I hope you will embrace the belief that you are the masters of your own destiny. Ogilvy PR will continue to provide a wonderful platform for you to perform, but you have to be part of building this platform. And as it is built, you need to work with your teams and your supervisors to figure out how you fit into the growing puzzle in a role that both advances you personally and also helps the firm. That is the gold standard in this business. Also, if there is something that upsets you about what we as a firm don't have nor do, please lead by example. Show us what you mean and how to do this with action. That is what I am trying to do with the North Asia business to serve as a model for the global network. We have a lot of assets and we have much work to do so please join me in being the model PR firm you would like to be part of today and tomorrow.

****

Get outside of your comfort zone, December 24, 2012

I am writing to you from beautiful South Africa in the middle of the bush. This morning my family and I tracked lions, elephants, wild dogs, zebras and buffalo. Yesterday we watched a mother rhino care for her children, and we sparred with monkeys who tried to steal our food. I hope all of you have a chance to experience a safari at some point in your life. On the ride I was thinking about how this relates to our lives at Ogilvy PR. I reflected on how fortunate we are that our "hunt" has thus far been so successful. I am thankful that we have such a robust environment for future food. I am aware that if we care for each other the road ahead of us is plentiful. I also thought about how important it is to get outside of our comfort zone to enjoy new environments and experience new stimuli.

So as I write the last *Monday Morning Mail* of 2012, I want to thank each and every one of you for your contribution. My only hope for all of us is that we keep this dream alive. We have wonderful clients whom we have done some very good work for, and we have a strong team that is formidable when we work together. And we are backed by, and very much part of, an incredibly strong Ogilvy brand name in this region. So there will be no individual call outs with this mail, but a collective shout out to all of you for 2012. We survived December 21, 2012, we are thriving towards the finish line, and as I write this with birds chirping in my ears I am enjoying the moment (with family as I hope all of you can do) and thinking about 2013. For those of you covering for the others on annual leave THANK YOU. I promise that we will cover for you too when it is your moment to take a breather. And I insist everyone must take a break.

The Western and Chinese New Years are just around the corner and this is a time for reflection and a period when you should make some commitments (resolutions) to yourself, your family and/or your co-workers. What are you going to do that is different next year from this year? What do you resolve to accomplish? My weight loss campaign was one of my resolutions that I went public with at the beginning of the year. To everyone who has reminded me of this, I want you to know I left Beijing at 87 kg, my target weight. I have fluctuated between 87 and 89 kg so this contest is not over. I will submit myself to a weigh-in on January 4, so stay tuned. This is only a start for me, however, and I hope to end 2013 in much better shape. Let's first get through January 4th.

Have a very happy holiday season and once again thank you for everything you have done. Please find time to get some rest and prepare to come back refreshed for an exciting 2013.

****

Speak less and do more in the Year of the Snake, February 18, 2013

A warm welcome back to everyone after a lengthy Lunar New Year break. We officially begin the Year of the Snake today. Let's work together to make it our best year ever.

As we begin the New Year let's make it one of "Deeds Not Words." Let's speak less and do more. Our work will speak for our creativity, our insight and our ability to execute. We are in a business that depends on our "brain" first and foremost. We need to exercise this and make sure our minds are healthy. At the same time our teams need to be comprised of people of all walks of life and all areas of strength. Also, we need "big hearts" to nurture our talent, embrace our clients and to build strong networks that form the foundation of any great public relations firm. And we need energy and optimism to make the impossible possible. Are you up for it? I certainly hope so. We need "deeds not words" to make this happen.

****

Organization

Accelerate now to maintain leadership position, March 4, 2013

Think Formula One racing for a moment. Racing experts explain most often the people who win Formula One championships are skillful at doing one thing. They accelerate around the course curves and take a leadership position. For Ogilvy PR in North Asia I would like us to think like a Formula One racer. We need to ACCELERATE NOW to maintain our leadership position. We must not be complacent. We must not let any obstacle stand in our way of winning, growing, doing more for our clients and taking care of our people. Today it is March 4. We are well into the new year, but it is still early. Winning new business and farming new assignments now can significantly impact our year. In fact all of the decisions we take now will determine how we do on December 31. In my personal opinion now it is more important than ever to win, execute and grow. We are past the Western and Chinese New Years and it is time to make our move. So please let's get stuck in and determined to accelerate our client campaigns, Ogilvy PR success and your own careers. Please do not put off until tomorrow what you can do today!

My second message is a plea to everyone to exercise better discipline in administering our business. I realize there are forms we must fill out, forecasts we must make and debt we must collect. Instead of detesting this (like I do), let's embrace it and make it our strength. We need more discipline about chasing and signing contracts, collecting debt, closing jobs, etc., and this is part of all of our jobs. We cannot escape this and unfortunately the more successful you are, the more disciplined administration is needed. So please let's collectively embrace this to ensure we are not only hugely successful, but also incredibly efficient in the process.

****

Client confidentiality, social media expertise and client retention, March 18, 2013

Whew! Last week was a doozy of a week filled with a mixture of emotions. On the hour I was celebrating one minute, concerned the following minute, comforted the next. I saw work and commitment from people that makes me very proud. I had a call with a client that ended a 15-year relationship we have with that client and while I knew this was coming, I was upset. And the minute that door closed, a number of other doors in significant new business opened. And that was my life this past week.

Monday Morning Mail

Three messages for this *Monday Morning Mail*. The first is the absolute importance of client confidentiality. I am working with a client now on an issue that arose when a confidential Ogilvy document made its way into the hands of a journalist. With the number of freelancers we have touching confidential information of our clients, we must be absolutely professional and disciplined in how this information is protected. There is going to be a lot of movement in the client security space and I expect everyone from Ogilvy to exhibit the utmost professionalism when it comes to client confidential information.

Second message relates to social media expertise and practices. Again, there is a lot of movement in the space. You must read the note I shared from Chris Graves last week about how not to cross the line. The world is focusing on China and Asia and the space for things to be done "under the radar" is gone. We must exhibit the utmost professionalism in everything we do. The test is this: if you were a client, would you trust yourself? Great PR is built on transparency, honesty and trust, and I expect that from everyone in Ogilvy PR in North Asia.

The third message is what I learned from the loss of our client. It is very clear to me that the closer we are with our clients, the better work we do. With this particular client, our distance grew and with the distance, we became dispensable. Hence client chemistry is vitally important. If you don't have some type of frequent contact with a client I promise you this is a recipe for termination. I personally believe in NO SURPRISES, meaning we should be so close to our clients and our people that there never should be news that shocks us. Do you feel you are close enough?

As a public relations firm that wants to lead the industry in North Asia - and the world - in the new era of public relations, we have a lot to do. Let's not forget that. But I am comforted in knowing that we have a very, very strong bunch of people with talent, commitment and the desire to be the very best.

****

Organization

Putting a price on core competence, April 15, 2013

I want to ask each of you today to think about what you do ... and what we do ... better than anyone else, and ask yourself would you pay your hourly rate for what you believe is your core competence? This is a familiar theme in these *Monday Morning Mails*, but the familiarity is there for a reason: It is central to our long-term success and existence.

I am writing to you on this Monday with mixed emotions. On one hand we have so much to celebrate. We have teams in Shanghai and Guangzhou that teamed to manage a huge potential crisis for a client and I am told our whole team did a wonderful job. We won a new client in the public affairs team without a pitch. Our Ogilvy PR Japan and China teams came together for a client seminar that I was told went very well. And, we just finished a huge weeklong event for a client handled by Ogilvy PR Beijing and H-Line Ogilvy Beijing with our global client leaving very pleased. So much to be proud of!

Yet, after six months of working around the globe – involving several offices - to bring Chengdu a creative idea, we were told it passed all approvals and in the last mile the idea got killed. Many offices spent much time on this and the campaign is now on ice. At the same time we have a client that we have worked with for two years in Beijing, who asked us to reconsider our fees. He has taken what he believes is strategic and brought it in house, and he has asked us to do what he feels is a commodity – execution of several external events - and reduced our fees by 2/3rds of their previous level. He wants to know if we will accept. We have not! While this client – a very smart, senior executive in his company - is not very familiar with the core of what we do, this request speaks to our relevance and how we could be perceived. The lesson is instructive in making sure that we are constantly assessing our true value and core competencies. So these events of the past week have been disappointing.

On top of this I am anxious and frustrated about our discipline in capturing the work we do in North Asia. This is my fault first and foremost. I am frustrated that I cannot call up on a moment's notice which people in Ogilvy PR are education PR experts, for example. That I cannot go to one place and get a client list of all of the education PR engagements we have done in North Asia for the past 10 years and review the engagement case studies. This takes discipline and a system for doing so and I am resolved to crack this. Ogilvy PR in North Asia needs to model fantastic knowledge management for this company and I am asking Ching Ping Yang and Ella Chan as the duel Chief Operating Officers in both Beijing and Shanghai to help us address this. Keep in mind that great knowledge management needs the discipline of everyone involved so all of you are critical to this.

So that's my rant. I am grateful to the people in this company who are dedicated to our clients' success and delight them every step of the way, and I want us all to think about how to build our core competency which becomes our insurance policy for our success in the future.

So thanks for all you do. We have so much going for us, but we need to think about our core competencies, we need to make sure we are not complacent, we need to be curious and we need to make sure that we are good to our clients, our staff and ourselves as a recipe to making us the best public relations agency in the North Asia market.

****

Success comes from being in 'the right place', May 6, 2013

"The Right Place."

I had two experiences this past week that represent how I am feeling about our business. The first was a new business opportunity for a very reputable organization. We had a few meetings with this Foundation and for some reason we just could not find our groove. I personally spent a lot of time trying to figure out the brief and what they wanted and I feel we still missed the mark. It reminds me of two things I feel we really need to work on.

First, all of us at Ogilvy PR do really well with a brief. We do well when we are given clear direction on what a client wants to do. But how often do we look at a client's challenge not from what they think they want, but what we as advisors think they should do? We need better diagnostic skills that get to the core of our clients' business problems and challenges and not just what a client says in their brief. This is all about the business ambition star in Fusion (Ogilvy's collaborative planning tool) and defining their challenge.

The second is that we often determine if a client is right or not for us if they have a "communications problem." But what I have learned from a lot of the recent valuable branding work our disciplined brothers and sisters are getting is that our branding recommendations are going beyond communications. They get to the heart of helping brands with their business problems and sometimes these problems or solutions are not an internal campaign, a press conference or a media interview. The solutions go much deeper into brand systems, channels, data analytics and more. I am not saying we depart from our core competency, but we need to know what this core competency is and how it relates to business today and tomorrow, and we need to acquire new skills to keep us relevant with where the world is going. I see that as my own leadership challenge for us, but everyone needs to do their share too with experimenting with new directions for our business. The success we are having with social@ogilvy is a start here. What's next?

The more upbeat experience I had was with a long-term staff member I evaluated this week. She is a Director and she was speaking glowingly about one of the fast-rising stars in her team. She said, this girl is in the "right place". She loves her job and it shows in her client work, in how much her team loves what they are doing and the success they are having. She said this one particular staff member smiles all the time and her work is fantastic. To me success in this business comes from being in the "right place." And as managers we have to help our people get into the right place. Finding that zone is like a fuel station for the mind, body and spirit. I certainly hope we can cultivate a culture where we help people find their "right places". If we do so we will all see the results in our work, our relationships and in our rewards.

****

Respect and discipline, September 9, 2013

I have two messages for this week's *Monday Morning Mail*. The first relates to the all important value of RESPECT. I have heard a few stories lately of instances where we as a firm were not respectful in terms of how we work with others. Respect comes in the form of how we talk to each other - and sometimes even what we don't say - and how we behave. Sitting in a training program answering your phone, texting and chatting throughout is not respectful. You may not recognize this and you may be working on clients' business, but totally tuning out and looking down at your phone is just not appropriate. You would be better off just excusing yourself. Arriving late to meetings in my opinion is also not respectful. I don't think we can use the traffic situation anymore as an excuse for being late. Traffic congestion is a reality in China and other North Asian markets. Taxis are sparse. Please be on time to meetings and appointments, period! Also, please build in some cushion around the start and finish of meetings so you can avoid being late. I have been in several meetings recently where Ogilvy PR folks arrive late and it is just not acceptable. What gives us the right to waste other people's time? This is a point of respect for other people and we must be leaders in the area of respect. Being respectful will also directly correlate to your success as a professional. We were in a pitch lately and I heard one of our competitors was disqualified because they arrived late to the pitch meeting and the European client was so angry he did not even accept their presentation. Be on time. Tune in. And please be respectful in all you do.

The second message I would like to share with you relates to DISCIPLINE. This is also connected to RESPECT in many ways. You need discipline in arriving to meetings on time and in changing behavior so you are seen as being more respectful. But the discipline I am writing to you about relates to the area of how we get things done and how you operate your professional life. I recently spoke to a WPP person who described Ogilvy as highly creative and very surprising (in a positive way), but also very loose. "At your best, you are the best," he said. "High energy. Very effective. At your worst, you are sloppy and disorganized." It made me think about what I believe makes this company great and that is the freedom and trust we have within Ogilvy. But that freedom and trust needs to be earned. We are not "time clock" watchers. We are not worried about when you come and when you go home, or what you do by and large. We believe you need a great deal of self discipline to operate your lives and your work. But there is absolutely no tolerance of abuse for the free and open privilege. And if you don't have the discipline in delivering for your teams, supervisors or clients, this is probably not the company for you. We do not like to discipline our employees. It does not make for a happy and productive environment and if we do it feels very bad for the supervisors as well. So please do me, you and your bosses a favor and discipline yourself so we don't ever have to have a difficult conversation with you.

****

Make the connection, November 11, 2013

One of the things that clearly differentiates us from others in our industry is our global network. While many of us toil in the day-to-day in our local markets we must not forget that we have at our fingertips decades of experience and expertise throughout the Ogilvy world. I was reminded of this last week with the visit to China of our Global Managing Director of Public Affairs, Jamie Moeller. Jamie has worked at Ogilvy PR for 26+ years and joined the company around the same time as me. In fact, I know Jamie well beyond our joint careers at Ogilvy as we are both from the same hometown in Michigan.

What comforted me during his visit was witnessing the time he spent with the Public Affairs practice in Beijing talking through tools and best practices and walking through potential clients with which we can work together.

With North Asia's thirst for creating global brands our network is clearly a differentiator. And I can promise you that we will be welcome with open arms when we deliver a ripe opportunity to the global network. This comes, however, with a challenge and that challenge rests with us to prepare our resident companies to properly expand globally. What we have found over the years is that some companies are more prepared than others and it takes a lot of communication and flexibility.

I also had a chance to visit our offices in Sydney, Australia two weeks ago. We are the market leader in Australia and the work the team is doing is first class. I met all of the leaders of the different businesses (we have a number of specialist firms in Australia) and experienced the lively Australian total-Ogilvy culture first hand. We share many clients with our colleagues down under and it is important we do not let the distance stand in the way of what we must do together.

My point here is that it is easy to come into the office everyday and do your thing in your local market. But we have a huge network around the world and you can grow personally and professionally by just connecting with others. The way networks net is not easy. It takes people willing to reach out and learn from other cultures and I would like us in North Asia to lead in the effort to be connected with Ogilvy partners throughout the world. As a first step why not go to the Ogilvy Intranet and find a colleague from another office and just introduce yourself and the work you do and make a connection?

This week's message: "Make the connection".

****

Monday Morning Mail

Industry-leading TICK - Talent, Invention, Clients and Knowledge, January 20, 2014

Priorities! This past week I was reminded of the importance of making priorities and ensuring the big "life game-changing priorities" take precedence. Andrew Thomas, President of Ogilvy PR in Southeast Asia & India, shared a story about something he learned from his heart surgeon brother-in-law. He described an exercise his brother-in-law did to explain life's priorities. His brother-in-law took a glass jar and began to fill it with big rocks. One-by-one he picked up a number of rocks, studied them and then placed each into the jar. When filled, he turned to Andrew and said, "this is full, right?" Andrew nodded in agreement. "Sure. Certainly looks filled to me." His brother-in-law then picked up a bag of sand. He opened the bag and poured it in left, right and center. He picked up the jar and shook it so that that sand filled the gaps throughout. "Is this full now?" Andrew smiled, ran his fingers through his full head of hair and responded, "wow, yes, it is certainly full now!" His brother-in-law then picked up a glass of water and poured the water in the jug filling it to the very top. He asked, "Is it full now?" "Yes, yes, yes," said Andrew. "It is now full." His brother-in-law then explained the point of the exercise. He said, "You see most people will tell you the meaning of this exercise is this: when you think your schedule is full and you can't squeeze another project or another minute in the day, there is always room for more. BUT THAT IS NOT THE POINT OF THE EXERCISE!" he counselled. "The point is this: if you don't put the big rocks into the jar first, there will never be room for them later."

To me this is such a simple story with a very important message: we must get our priorities right or we will never have time for those "big rocks" in life. So with this *Monday Morning Mail* I am encouraging us all to make sure we all have our "big rocks" identified as we start the year.

I am beginning this Monday fully charged. I spent the last week with colleagues from around Asia. The first part of the week the Ogilvy PR leadership team throughout the region gathered to discuss our future. We are blessed with great leadership in our company and I truly believe we can do anything we put our minds to. The second part of the week was spent with our "Pacesetters", a collection of Ogilvy staffers that are part of Ogilvy PR's next-level leaders. We had a full three days together and this team of colleagues was really most impressive.

The week-long conference theme was "Change and Exchange." We talked about the changes that are taking place and how we are going to lead them. Front foot, proactive, opportunity assault was the order of the week. We also had time to exchange a lot of views on how best to run our business in each of our markets. Finally, we rolled out an initiative called TICK you will hear more about. The TICK initiative is all about what we are going to do to lead the industry in Talent, Invention, Clients and Knowledge.

****

Simplicity, Advocacy, Muscle and Effort (SAME), June 23, 2014

I write this *Monday Morning Mail* feeling very competitive. In between meetings and emails and everything else we do, I have been following the World Cup. If you have been watching this you would know that there are many surprises in this World Cup. Spain is out. Italy lost to Costa Rica this weekend. As of 7:50 this a.m. the US is still in the running with a 2-2 tie to Portugal. Our Asia Pacific countries are doing well. Despite Australia's losses, the team played two fine matches in the group of death and played very well against the Dutch. Japan and Korea are still in the running and have opportunities. My condolences to our England colleagues. In this World Cup the English have experienced the bitter taste of defeat, and it is a meal we must avoid at all costs!

So in the spirit of the World Cup I am writing to all of you with a cautionary message and that is this: "We Must Fight Against Sameness!"

I am using the acronym SAME because that is what I fear and I hear from our clients. They often comment, "You people in the PR business are all the same! Surprise me and give me something different."

How to be different? Let's embrace the concept of sameness head on and blow the F@#* out of our competition. What do I mean?

S stands for simplicity. We must work very hard to explain our ideas, processes and systems in simple, easy-to-understand language. In meeting after meeting, when I do pitch reviews, our client feedback is that we are much too complicated. I heard a client on Friday tell me that he feels Ogilvy is very smart. He knows we are good. But we make things more complicated than they have to be. We were defeated on a recent global pitch because we were just more complicated than a competitor who presented a very similar concept... simply. We must be creative, insightful, strategic and thorough. But we must not complicate ideas. We need to present them in clean and concise ways. S stands for simplicity.

Monday Morning Mail

A stands for advocacy. At the heart of what we do at Ogilvy PR is build advocates to drive business results. Whether it is in the traditional or social media space, in executing any of the products we have at our disposal, in carrying out best practices in our industry, we cultivate advocates. One could argue that advocacy is the most effective and credible means to drive behavior change and this is our area to own. You will hear more about this but please do think of what we do in the context of building advocacy for our clients.

M stands for muscle. Lots of people and clients like to sell against us because of the size and perceived complexity of the Ogilvy Group. We're an easy target. We must not let anyone do that to us. Our size and resources give us muscle. We must use it to our advantage. There are so many smart people at this company doing many different things. At our best I don't think anyone can compete with us if we work as a team. Let's do our best to utilize the total resources of the Ogilvy Group. We are clearly distinguished by our size and success and we need to leverage that to make sure we win at all costs.

E stands for effort. We must put in the effort to win. Without proper effort, a bit of sweat and tears, we won't get there. Think Luis Suarez of Uruguay who said he had a barbaric desire to destroy England. Think Spain and the concept of sameness which led to their defeat. Many of their players claimed they just didn't have the heart this year. As a network we have won a lot, and we must never ever forget the euphoric feeling of "winning". Without effort, I fear we will slip into the pool of sameness and mediocrity that is occupied by many of our competitors.

So that's my message for this week. Embrace and fight sameness. We can do so by being Simple, focusing on Advocacy, using our Muscle and giving 110% Effort. And with that we will be different in a sea of competition that has a few stars but nothing of the breadth and depth of Ogilvy PR.

****

A nudge or a shove in preparation for 2015, September 9, 2014

Dear Colleagues,

A gentle "nudge" or a huge "shove" - take your pick. "Nudge" is the theme of this week's *Monday Morning Mail*. "Nudge" was the theme of the regional executive committee (REGCO) meeting held this past week in Thailand hosted by our regional leaders Paul Heath and Kent Wertime. "Nudge" is what Paul and Kent are asking everyone in the REGCO to do to finish the next four months of the year. We are having a very strong year and most units are doing very well, but we need to nudge up other units that need some help. Paul and Kent's ask of everyone was to share a nudge from their responsibilities to boost us up a bit more for this year and next.

As most of you know Paul and Kent are very gentlemanly and their "Nudge" asks were a polite way of saying "let's all do a little bit better, improve ourselves a bit more" and be true to David Ogilvy's "Divine Discontent." As I sat through the two days I was thinking to myself how great it would be to see everyone live up to the spirit of their "Nudge" promises, and in some parts of our business I was thinking we need a huge "shove". What does this mean to you? In reviewing how you prepare yourself, your teams, your areas of responsibility for today and tomorrow, if incremental improvement is all you need, join the nudge initiative. And if you think you need a bit more than just a nudge, give yourself a huge shove. Stay tuned for my nudge, shove asks of you all in this next four months as we prepare for 2015.

****

Culture eats strategy for breakfast, October 20, 2014

"Culture eats strategy for breakfast!" This was the comment from the Mary Kay CMO when I told her how impressed I was with her company's special culture. Mary Kay has a very loyal employee community worldwide and they put great emphasis on the people who make up Mary Kay. Her comment reminded me of many of my own experiences at Ogilvy. The culture we have in Asia is very distinct and I hope we nurture this in everything we do. We need to make sure we cultivate the best environment for our client brands to succeed and for our people to excel with limited obstacles. This is not easy, but it needs to be at the core of everything we are about.

Attending the Mary Kay beauty contest event was the most memorable. At the end of the event the whole audience, some 300+ people, stood up and started singing and dancing to the Mary Kay theme song. I looked left and there was our own Shanghai Managing Director, Ella Chan, dancing and waving her hands in the air. Mary Kay is a very large client of our Shanghai office and Ella Chan leads this. You could see the client love in her celebratory dance. The senior clients came over to me to tell me how much they loved our team and how great of a partner we were. Mary Kay is a team effort between ourselves and the client and there is no question why this client is in such a healthy state. The team loves working on this and it certainly shows. I got the same feedback from the other meetings I had. When we come together in true partnership with our clients, the results are most often outstanding for everyone. So thank you everyone who works on these clients. If you don't have a trusting, close relationship with your client, that is a warning sign to get in front of them and do something extraordinary.

Last week …I also caught up with a young staffer from our Hong Kong office who has been with us for more than five years. She reached out just to have a chat. I was delighted because I know of her, but I didn't know a lot about her. She said as she hits her five-year mark she wanted to just have a chat about her career. She is self-motivated and outside of work does charity work and self-improvement study. I am so happy she connected with me. For all of you who think often about your career plans I encourage you to reach out to your supervisors and/or to someone you respect to chat about the future. My advice to this colleague was to think first and foremost about what she wants for herself. To become her own brand manager. If she identifies what she wants for herself, the time spent at work on some of the minutia we have to take care of is tolerable. I told her I only hope her plan involves Ogilvy and the big platform this company gives us to address our dreams. A very welcomed and enjoyable conversation. The materials we have on "The Brand Called You" I shared with her are below. Both are a bit dated, but worthwhile reviewing nonetheless.

So thank you for all you do. You are what makes up the Ogilvy culture. "Culture eats strategy for breakfast!"

****

Leadership

Taking a leadership lesson from our founder, David Ogilvy.

Chapter Four

Leadership

Trumpeter Swans, July 7, 2008

Dear Friends,

Tomorrow marks one month away from the Olympics and things are heating up in Beijing. On Friday adidas opened the largest retail outlet they have anywhere in the world in Beijing and this was the feature of a full-page Wall Street Journal article on Thursday. Congratulations adidas team. For the Olympics, Ogilvy PR is helping with the Swiss House, the Brazil House, J&J's Pavilion, and activation for adidas, UPS, Bank of China (H-Line Ogilvy) and more. We are entering the final phase of preparations and things are getting exciting.

The big news though is that the PA team and I have been working on a proposal to represent the Chengdu Government with their earthquake recovery efforts. On Monday of last week Joe and I met the Mayor and we were confirmed as their partner. This involves media training, media monitoring and outreach at first, and we have a real chance to help them given the Mayor's open and earnest approach. We'll keep you informed as to how this goes.

Thanks to all of you as well who responded to the Trumpeter Swan question. The intention was not to get the actual definition (as to be honest I did not know the Trumpeter Swan existed), but lo and behold I received a ton of different definitions, all very interesting. I did ask as the Trumpeter Swan was something David Ogilvy put in a recruitment advertisement to recruit people to Ogilvy. Here's an explanation:

David Ogilvy - "Trumpeter Swans" – those who combine personal genius with inspiring leadership.

The late advertising genius David Ogilvy used these words to describe the talent he was seeking: "... rare trumpeter swans capable of inspiring a motley crew of writers and artists; they must be sure-footed judges for a wide range of different products; they must be good presenters; and they must have a colossal appetite for midnight oil."

Leadership

Environmental Tip of the Week

Thanks to Walker Frost for this week's Environmental Tip:

China's Ministry of Science and Technology has published a handbook on ways the public can reduce energy use and emissions. One way is to turn off your air conditioning three minutes before you leave the house, rather than as you walk out the door. At a conservative estimate, one person doing this would save 5 kWh (kilowatt-hours) of electricity a year and reduce CO_2 emissions by 4.8 kg (kilograms). If all the users of China's 150 million air-conditioning units did the same, 750 million kWh of electricity could be saved annually, with CO_2 emissions reduced by 720,000 tonnes.

Have a good week and a happy July 4th!

Scott

****

Apples, insights and mad inventors, December 1, 2008

Dear Friends,

On this Monday following what is known in North America as "Thanksgiving Weekend", I want to thank you - each and every one of you - for the contribution you make to this company. I am personally living my dream working with all of you in this dynamic industry, in one of the fastest-growing countries and regions in the world, in a Group company that prizes creativity, bravery, curiosity and results. For those of you who don't know, Thanksgiving is a holiday where we take time out to give thanks for the blessings we received during the year. It normally takes place in the fall and historically relates to giving thanks for plentiful crops, but has evolved into a weekend family gathering that takes time out for appreciating everything one has in life. So thank you!

I read a great passage in a book this week by Jeremy Bullmore, a famous advertising man, non-executive Director of WPP and the copywriter of many of the WPP Annual Reports. A book was published about his pieces in the

WPP Annual Reports called, "Apples, Insights and Mad Inventors." Anyway, in one of his articles he comments about the role of two apparently contradictory forces in high-performing communications companies: one is the need for order and process and routine; and the other is the requirement of creative anarchy. Somehow, he points out, great companies foster both. He uses a description of this from EF Schumacher's 1973 classic, "Small is Beautiful", where he talks about corporate organizations:

"Without order, planning, predictability, central control, accountancy, instructions to the underlings, obedience, discipline - without these nothing fruitful can happen, because everything disintegrates. And yet - without the magnanimity of disorder, the happy abandon, the entrepreneurship venturing into the unknown and incalculable, without the risk and the gamble, the creative imagination rushing in where bureaucratic angels fear to tread - without this, life is a mockery and a disgrace."

What this reminded me of was the importance we must place on discipline, policies and order. And what we all must do to embrace the spirit of creativity that must live and prosper for us to be successful. And it reminded me of our great strength in this country - our size and scale and resources - and our great challenge to be "Big and Small." To make sure that we make the best of our "bigness", while also being "small": operating quickly and intensely focused on our clients.

The second is shared from Daniel Cheng, our Director of Talent & Development in Asia. He shared the following with all of the leaders of our businesses. I think this is relevant for everyone here. Are you a bad boss and how can you change?

Habits of a Bad Boss

> *Change your mind. Change it several times a day.*
> *Be sure your employees don't know what's important to you.*
> *If you don't like it, you don't like it. You don't have to explain.*
> *Bring your employees along to all your meetings. But don't let them speak.*
> *Thank your employees - but only for efforts below their skill level.*
> *Schedule weekly "all hands" meetings that require half the employees to travel (to you, of course).*
> *Ask your tech savvy employees to take time from their projects to set up your home computer, preferably when the maid is there.*
> *Agree to deadlines and then accelerate them.*
> *Schedule "critical" meetings a few days before Christmas.*

Leadership

Send emails at 2am. On Sunday. Mark them urgent.

Be careful not to get too wrapped up in your employees' own goals.

****

Note from Maggie, December 22, 2008

Dear All,

We have the honor to hear today from someone I respect very, very much in this market. I have known Maggie Tsai for the better part of the last seven years and have watched her work her magic for the past six years. She is a professional that combines smarts with hard work, she has a special way of dealing with people and she is extremely reliable. I have often described her as someone very soft on the outside, but like a tiger on the inside. We can all learn from her. She has served at the helm of H-Line Ogilvy since its founding. Both she and Henry Huang created a sister company that I am personally honored to serve. And she has attracted hundreds of staff that help deliver huge results for some of China's biggest brands. I asked Maggie to share her thoughts on the past, present and future. And, in a departure from our normal format, this is just a "note from Maggie." Onwards and upwards, Maggie.

Scott

Note from Maggie

Since the onset of the financial crisis, I think we have heard enough about cost controls, headcount freezes, salary cuts and lay-offs. Almost all enterprises are proactively or reactively taking actions to hone their competitive edge so that they can emerge stronger out of the crisis.

However, I wonder if we, as individuals, have thought about what we can personally do faced with such a crisis, apart from panicking, holding on job transfers or wait-and-see.

Next year, we will certainly enjoy more leisure time than we did in this past Olympic Year (although certainly not as idle as during the months of SARS in 2003). Next year, we will also be more thrifty and careful while spending. Still, 2009 can be a memorable year – as long as right at the outset, we creatively use our PR minds to design and drive another "bumper year".

How do we do that? I have a few quick suggestions, and you are welcome to chip in more ideas:

How?

Spend some time to think through our priorities in life: When it's busy, we can hardly afford the luxury of spare time to take a moment and think. We can now finally slow down a little bit and ponder - if life were to end shortly, what is it that we always really wanted to accomplish before we went away on that final journey? I've heard many a friend say: I want to make a fortune so that I can take good care of my parents. I've also witnessed sorrow and regrets over the loss of parents when people thought they had finally earned enough to give their parents a great life. The irony is that we naturally worry about immediate things like the financial crisis, but we usually misperceive our life as perpetual, thus neglecting such priorities as health and emotional life.

Be grateful for what we have and take actions to show our gratitude: Family members and teachers naturally come to mind when we think about thanks-giving. But the sky is not home to the North Star or the Great Bear only; it is the myriad nameless stars that light up the heavenly space. Do you still remember the perfect stranger who offered you the shelter of an umbrella in pouring rain? Are you grateful to the migrants who toil day and night to spruce up our city? Or notice that wild flower at your front door, or that bird on the twig, chirping away cheerfully? We should be sensitive to these trivial things in life, be thankful, and pass on the warmth through maybe a simple thank-you to the restaurant waiter or for instance, by giving up our seat to an elderly person on a crowded bus.

Be more creative: Crisis is a good time for creative ideas because now, more than any time before, clients would require us to think out of the box. It is said wafer biscuit was invented during an economic slowdown when consumers reduced spending on chocolate. It became an immediate market hit because it retains the taste of chocolate but is sold at a lower price. Similarly, we should excel with our creativity to showcase Ogilvy's strategy-based proposals and value-add.

Extensive reading: Read a good book each week (to expand our horizons, I would suggest to restrict the number of fiction to within 20%). After a year, we would have read 52 new books. I would suggest exchanging the info on good reads with friends or at reading clubs. We will not only become more knowledgeable, but our horizons would also be dramatically broadened.

Leadership

Life-long learning: *Piece together fragments of time to take a course (e.g. spoken English) or develop a hobby (e.g. Yoga); and most importantly, keep at it! We should make full use of the hard-to-come-by luxury of time during this financial crisis. Once we go back to our busy schedule, we'll regret not having utilized our free time properly when we had it.*

I feel my note is becoming more like a New Year Resolution. But I strongly believe the current crisis will be over much quicker than we expect – just like how distant SARS feels today. The good thing is that the financial crisis has only started. It is not too late if we start planning now. I hope my note comes just in time.

Finally, I would like to wish everyone a most joy-filled holiday season!

Maggie

****

Ouch! An example of miscommunication... November 30, 2009

Dear Colleagues:

We must never forget we are in the communications business. We are hired to help our clients communicate better. To send messages that resonate with their target audience groups. Below is a paragraph (I cannot make this up) from a company CEO to his global team. This company is less than successful and, by the way this guy communicates, you can see why. Here is a paragraph from a global note he sent:

> *"A small task force of our senior leaders has determined the best path forward that capitalizes on our original vision and investment, while forging a strategy that is sustainable and competitively differentiating. We are focused on a large and attractive opportunity around global marcom activation and delivery that allows us to build upon our core technology and infrastructure assets (e.g., DAM, Brandshares, content management, etc.) as well as our global resource base to bring diverse campaigns to market more quickly, effectively and cost-efficiently than most current industry players."*

Ouch! Let's remember we are in the communications business and we must communicate.

****

Monday Morning Mail

Leadership and management, September 3, 2012

Dear Friends,

Leadership and Management: both are important for thriving businesses. Not all great leaders are necessarily good managers though, and vice versa. To me, leadership is about the ability to define the future path of an organization and make the necessary decisions to pave the road of that path. Management is about making sure the whole organization is together in following that path in an effective, efficient and happy way. These are not textbook definitions, but that's how I look at the both of them.

****

Damned if you do, damned if you don't, August 26, 2013

My topic for this week's *Monday Morning Mail* is "Leadership". Leadership is a subject I have been interested in throughout my career and it touches on much of what we do in public relations. I have studied what makes great leaders, and also questionable moves made by some people in leadership positions that undermined their ability to lead. In many ways when you are a leader you are "damned if you do and damned if you don't"; half of the people will support a particular decision, another half will not. There are many definitions of leadership, styles and philosophies, but this is not what this note is about. This message is about two experiences I have had in my career that have shaped my thinking on leadership.

The first experience comes from a meeting I was part of this past Thursday and Friday led by Paul Heath, our regional Group CEO. TB, Steve Dahllof and Chris Reiterman were also part of this meeting. The discussion was around defining actions to take to make Ogilvy as an agency quicker, stronger, smarter and more effective. It centered around clients and their needs in this new era of marketing, the Ogilvy arsenal, and how to maximize this and lead the industry as demands shift. The good news is that much of what you and I may worry about daily, the leadership of this firm is worrying about too. And instead of just letting it fester, you will see moves that experiment with discipline-neutral teams, digital acceleration, data, best practices in talent development and more. While nothing earthshaking resulted from this meeting, I was comforted in participating in this and knowing that our leadership in this region is not passive. There is a movement to make our strength in size and resources work to our advantage in shaping the future for the industry. It was about being on our front foot and on offense; not on our back foot and on defense. I always loved the quote from the management guru, Peter Drucker: "the best way to your future is to create it." It felt like we were creating our future in Hong Kong on Thursday and Friday.

The second experience comes from lessons I have learned from TB and Shenan, the Chairman and CEO of the Ogilvy Group in Greater China respectively. I have worked with both TB and Shenan for 22 years and there are few people I trust more than the both of them. They lead Ogilvy in Greater China with an incredible degree of humanity, and they know that getting the most out of creative people from different walks of life is about giving them room to create and to trust them. Beyond anything work related they did for me, I remember 22 years ago needing to get my passport out of a police station in Taiwan at midnight (for visa reasons) because I had to make an urgent trip to the US. They pulled out all stops to make that happen. I remember when I worried about the repercussions of having a senior person leave and TB coached me not to worry. He explained that although they will go and it would create some short-term pain, in the end they would spread the Ogilvy gospel and it would be OK. That senior person left and came back. Most of all I learned there are no secrets to great leadership. If you treat people how you want to be treated, everything will be OK.

Since being named as Steve's successor to begin January 1, 2014, I am reflecting on a lot of these things. How we collectively lead the PR industry in the next several years is very dear to me and I hope you are feeling as excited as I am.

****

The best way to predict the future is to create it, October 31, 2013

From the day I was selected to follow Steve in the APAC CEO role I have been thinking about what is next for us in Ogilvy PR. Steve has navigated and led the Ogilvy PR ship so well and he leaves very big shoes to fill. Not to mention more stylish shoes as Steve is regarded as being much more fashionable than me. What I cannot promise is that I am going to be as well dressed as Steve, but I will try to set a new course for us as we enter the next era of the PR industry in Asia. As I am contemplating this, Chris Graves, our Global CEO, sent over these notes that are part of the broader themes shaping our world. Please do read this when you have a moment as they are important to each and everyone of us. I am thinking through these themes and others as we set the agenda for Asia. Please also think about what role you will play in the new PR dynamic.

Lately I have also been thinking a lot about our approach to new business. We are nearly two months away from the end of the year and there is a lot of guess work going on about whether one client will choose us in a competitive pitch, or whether the brief that has been provided to us by a prospective client is real. Honestly, I usually feel that once we get into November and December the year is almost over and we should stop hoping and face reality. I still have some hope out there for the forecasts each of you have provided, but that is waning daily. One thing I have learned over the last few months is that we need to be much better at forecasting, phasing and resource planning, and I hope to introduce some measures in the coming year to help us do that. With that said, we have a ton of new business opportunities in front of us and I remain convinced that "what we do, and what we don't do is equally important." Hence, being prudent in choosing what we go for and doing our best to gain "unfair advantage" is all the more important.

As far as managing the future and winning new business is concerned, I love to reflect on a quote once communicated by the management guru Peter Drucker. I have written about this before, but this quote reflects how I think about the importance of managing our fate: "The best way to predict the future is to create it." - Peter Drucker.

****

Leadership

Everyday leadership, January 6, 2014

On this first Monday morning of 2014 I am writing the beginning of a series of *Monday Morning Mail*s I plan to send to you every other week. This is a tradition I began in China and was extended to North Asia two years ago with the objective of keeping everyone informed at Ogilvy PR about other Ogilvy happenings in the region. It has also served as my own platform to share views on life, our industry, the world and other topics. It is not mandatory reading, but I hope people will read it to stay informed. The *Monday Morning Mail* has also served as a chance for me to share many of the interesting presentations, documents, files, papers and more that make their way into my inbox.

I have been thinking a lot about this new role. Under Steve's leadership this network has thrived. In 2013 we won a lot of awards, secured some very healthy new business and grew respectably in most offices. We really have a great thing going. Yet, we are not immune from challenges. The industry is changing at lightning speed and we have to embrace and lead the change. We have 1,000+ people in the network, but we often work independently without leveraging the very best we have in all of our offices. We have a wonderful brand that brings us new opportunities, but what about the prospective clients who don't reach out to us but could use our services? We have people in offices from all walks of life, both men and women, at all ages: are we providing the best opportunities for these people to deliver what truly moves them? One friend of mine who worked at McKinsey & Company told me McKinsey has a belief that they don't do career pathing. The stars "find their own McKinsey." I would like to think that Ogilvy PR is a place where anyone could "find their own Ogilvy." A place where you can create a role that is both fulfilling for yourself, and one that also provides value to the company, our clients and colleagues. That is really the gold standard in managing your own careers. We have a lot to do in the area of inventing new products to help all of the offices lead the industry and in knowledge management so that cases, credentials, bios and more are at your fingertips.

We are in such a good place... yet there is so much to do. I am humbled by the opportunity to lead this network and I promise that I will do my very best to ensure we maximize opportunities for our people, our clients and the company in an effort to maintain our leadership position. I am open and accessible and can be reached on this email address by anyone. There are so many things we should and can do, and it is up to us to define them. So if anyone at Ogilvy PR has an idea that you would like considered, please do share this. I am very much looking forward to visiting the offices around the region and meeting all of you.

For this first *Monday Morning Mail* for the Asia Pacific region, I am sharing one of my favorite speeches made by Shelly Lazarus, Chairman Emeritus of Ogilvy & Mather, entitled, "Everyday Leadership." Shelly gave this to Deloitte Consulting more than a decade ago and its messages continue to be highly relevant today.

****

Benevolence, generosity and leadership, June 9, 2014

As you read this on Monday morning I will be deep into our regional Exco meeting in Shanghai led by Paul Heath, together with all of the regional leaders from the Ogilvy Group. While I do not enjoy lots of "full-day conference room" meetings about what we are going to do, I enjoy these meetings very much. These meetings provide a venue to sit, reflect on what we are doing, hear what others are working on and debate about the future and what we must do. I find comfort in knowing that we have discipline in the region to chart the course for the future, and we are very much a part of this. The comfort ends when we enter the room because not everything is polite, but the intent is pure and that is to chart the course for your futures and mine and for Ogilvy's success in Asia Pacific. To me, this is part of leadership.

And "Leadership" is the theme of this week's *Monday Morning Mail*. Leadership is a broad topic that has many different angles and aspects. I want to touch on the combination of benevolence and generosity and their relevance to leadership in today's dispatch.

Why benevolence and generosity? Because these past two weeks I spent my time with many leaders, and I was trying to think of what was the common defining characteristic amongst all of them. What was top of mind was their kindness and generosity, and how this was central to how they live their lives.

Among the people I met were the one and only Pele. This guy is a leader in the world of football (known as soccer for us American novices!). What struck me about Pele was his kindness in spending time with my children and me before he left Beijing for the airport. This was the tail end of his trip, he had signed thousands of autographs and taken hundreds of photos, and he was in no hurry to get to the airport. He was everything you would envision him to be in serving as the king of football. He is a leader and his leadership star is very high right now with the world cup kicking off in Brazil this coming week. I was moved by his benevolence and he was everything I imagined about him and more.

So my ask to all of us at Ogilvy PR is to never forget the importance of being generous. If we want to remain as leaders we must perfect the core of what we are about. And that core is about doing the right thing and taking the time to help colleagues, friends, staff and clients. I hope we as an organization participate in random acts of kindness often. And by doing so, we will become the Pele of the communications profession.

One other thing I learned about Pele's story is that he has been taken advantage of by many people over the years. Let's remember in business we must be generous and honest, but we also must make sure the people we are dealing with have the same values.

OK, enough preaching. Be generous and be smart. Don't worry about the return. "What goes around comes around!" and let's lead the way.

****

The greatest professionals love serving clients.

Chapter Five

Client Service

Curiosity is at the heart of great PR people, June 2, 2008

I want to begin by thanking those of you who have provided feedback to the earlier *Monday Morning Mail*s, who have read the articles and who take time to think about how to improve themselves in our profession. Curiosity is at the heart of great public relations people, and it is what defines all of the great O&Mers I have known.

Week in Review

This past week featured our hero team supporting the Asia Society Conference in Tianjin, which was kicked off by Vice President Xi Jiping. Our support of the Asia Society follows on the heels of Ogilvy PR handling PR for the Women's Conference in Shanghai last month, and precedes our support of an environmental conference later in June in Beijing. We're also slated to help with the World Economic Forum in Tianjin in late September. Many of you may ask why we do so many of these conferences? Well, they provide us with the ability to place our clients in prime speaking slots, they give us access to the media at these conferences and overall they have had reciprocal impact on our reputation. I am grateful for all of the teams who contribute to these, and who will be involved in the future. If you want to know more about our conference involvement, feel free to email me and I will put you in touch with the project teams.

This week also saw the launch of the famous UPS *Asian Business Monitor*. As I flew around China this week, I saw references in both local and international media. In fact, there were two pieces in the *Asian Wall Street Journal*. The *Asian Business Monitor* is a great campaign for UPS led by Ogilvy PR in Hong Kong that positions UPS as the authority on global trade by taking the temperature in a survey of small and mid-sized business to probe their views on the future prospects of trade within Asia and globally.

Interesting Read

This week's article is an unusual entry, but something that I became very interested in. It is an article from the *International Herald Tribune* about

Barrack Obama's personal aide, Reggie Love. Why did this interest me? Well, because this is a human interest story about people surrounding US presidential contender - Obama - and I think it was an interesting public relations play. The campaign team obviously recognized the personal power of having a young, popular former football player as Obama's personal assistant and it is a human interest story that says more about the people in the Obama team. It's a softer piece and a good read and represents the lighter side of the campaign. If you have time, read this with a lens that asks... why did they choose to feature this guy, at this time, and how did they do it?

> ### Environmental Tip of the Week
>
> This week's environment request is quite simple. Could we ask everyone to keep a set of their own chopsticks (plastic, or whatever) so that we don't need to use the wooden ones that come with take out? For some this may seem to be ridiculous, but the disposable chopsticks do add up and we certainly want to be good environment citizens.

****

The devil is in the details, June 10, 2008

Dear Colleagues,

I realize today's *Monday Morning Mail* is reaching you on Tuesday. I certainly hope you had a good Dragon Boat Festival. Last week featured a number of discussions and renewal of a key client contract for China. There were a few issues that came up in this client conversation that I think are important to note related to quality, and these discussions came through in other client work this week as well. In the client review, in comparing one team to another, the positive comments were: 'this person understands the industry'... 'this person has strong media relations'... 'this person has strong execution skills and finds new ways to do things.' The negative comments: 'this team just goes through the motions'... 'there is no added value provided by this person'... 'this team is just sloppy in its execution.' So my advice for us at this mid-year point:

Client Service

Take professional services guru David Maister's advice. That is: 'A client does not care how much you know, until they know how much you care.'

- you have to care.

- how can you bring added value? Here I believe you have to get out from behind your desk and have conversations. With journalists. Third parties. Others. Try to get a sense of what is happening in the external market and feed it in to your client. Unsolicited.

- mind the details. As I travel through the Ogilvy PR offices, many people look like they just rolled out of bed. You want respect? Dress the part. Show up on time. Make sure your documents look professional. Do the paperwork well. Proofread your documents and emails. Make sure you send attachments when you say you will. Don't misspell your client's name. Friends, the devil is in the details and you must get this right.

- check in with your clients regularly. In my view there should never be any surprises if you are in touch with your clients on an ongoing basis.

- never be dishonest. In my view, great client relationships are built on trust and having open, honest dialogue and following through is the only way to build trust.

Environmental Tip of the Week

Shared by our colleagues in Guangzhou, the staff are using handkerchiefs to save the use of tissues in the office. Every bit helps here. If you have a frequent runny nose, and you are a heavy user of tissues, let me know. I will personally buy you a handkerchief.

****

Monday Morning Mail

Treat confidentiality very seriously, July 14, 2008

Dear Friends,

Good morning. We are now 25 days away from the big day. Are you as excited as I am? And while the environment in Beijing is rather peaceful now (a bit cloudy)... that will soon change in the days to come. The Olympic teams at Ogilvy PR are especially burning the midnight oil and the event we've been waiting for for the past seven years is upon us. "Jiayou* China!"

This week I had the pleasure of sitting in the H-Line Ogilvy mid-year management meeting. As I sat there and listened to what they are doing with the media, looking at Louis Luo's digital presentation and more, I felt a bolt of energy. Why? Because there is so much to be shared amongst us all. Where Ogilvy PR can help with media training and foreign media liaison and more, there is a ton of great resources and thinking from H-Line Ogilvy as well. We need to find the areas where we can cooperate and share, and those where we don't for competitive reasons. But what is clear to me is that there is a ton of great resources in this company!

I also personally was involved in a bittersweet lesson this week. As the lead on a regional project, I failed to advise one market in Asia about sensitivities in talking about a new client assignment. One of the account managers sent out an email mentioning we were working with the client and it created a bit of an issue. The lesson here is this: Our clients come to Ogilvy because they "trust us". That trust is a very strong statement and goes beyond any contracts that we can write with them. Above all we must nurture that trust and do the right thing for our clients. That is the way we can strengthen our relationships. So, we must treat confidentialities very seriously and we must let our clients know that "we care" and we are looking after them.

Also, an Ogilvy alum returned from the US to visit us. Ben Levy is his name and he is in a 10-year fellowship at Harvard studying the migration of Han Chinese into the Xinjiang area in the 18th and 19th century. I had a great lunch with him. He is here reading the ancient Manchu scripts in the Forbidden City archives. It reminds me that there are people doing vastly different things than us and we must make the time to have conversations of totally different natures to learn and grow. The conversation was fascinating.

*jiayou (加油) literally means 'add oil'; used idiomatically to mean 'make an all-out effort'

> ### Environmental Tip of the Week
>
> Organize your refrigerator in such a way that the objects you use most often are the most accessible. Also, after you have used items from the refrigerator, don't put them away one by one but rather group them all on the kitchen counter and put them back in the fridge all at once. These simple habits will cut down on the amount of time spent with the refrigerator door open, ultimately saving you money and bringing more "blue sky days."

****

The delicate balance between managing expectations and overdelivery, July 28, 2008

Dear Friends,

A wonderful "blue-sky" morning to you all. We are 11 days away from the big day and counting.

The Past Week

I want to address an issue in today's note that I believe is important to all of us as we develop our professional client servicing and management skills. That issue is "the management of expectations." Why? Because this week I spent a lot of time with staff addressing miscommunication or "expectation" issues, and with a client frustrated because they expected results that were different than what they got and, in my opinion, nearly impossible.

As everyone is so busy what happens is that we get on with work, but fail to do the necessary communication around what is expected and by when. I personally believe in overcommunication to ensure everyone is on the same page. If you know what you need to do, by a certain date, and how the work should be presented, stress levels go down and you can work to deliver above and beyond expectations. We need to spend the time in management and with our staff to do such things so that we can always deliver beyond expectation.

There is one wrinkle with all of this, however. And that is if we work to manage the expectations of our clients, and we try to manage them in such a way that they feel we are not committing to doing industry-leading work, they will find another partner that tells them they can achieve the results. So there is a careful balance here. We need to think about the language we use, not commit, but let our clients know that we will kill ourselves delivering more than expected.

This whole topic of "management" of expectations can be a huge recipe for success for us. As managers we need all of you to be happy and to trust that we will work in your best interests, and our clients need to trust us and know that we are honest people who will work to deliver outstanding results. Please, more communication than less will get us here.

The big development of the week is that Ogilvy PR has been named the Asia Pacific Consultancy of the Year by Paul Holmes of the prestigious Holmes Report. The honor was based on a survey of more than 50 local and international firms operating in the APAC region. In the words of Marcia Silverman, "These are tremendous accolades for the agency as our Asia-Pacific network continues to lead the region in all aspects from size, to awards, to new specialist practice creation."

Environmental Tip of the Week

Reduce "standby power" (the energy used while an appliance is switched off or not performing) at home and at work. The easiest way is to unplug appliances that are not being used. You can also plug your appliances into power surge protector strips (with multiple electrical outlets) and turn the power off at the entire strip.

Throughout August we will dedicate the *Monday Morning Mail*s to Olympic marketing in the spirit of the Games of the XXIX Olympiad.

Onwards and upwards,

Scott

****

Client Service

The importance of accurate forecasting, September 22, 2008

While the new business is flowing in, we must also look after our existing business first and foremost. So please remember, the best way to grow our business is to do good work for our existing clientele.

This Past Week

Ogilvy is entering its budget sessions these next two months and the management team is busy putting together projections for next year. Being able to forecast well is a very important skill as you become a manager, and this is what seems to be the key challenge for next year. With the challenges to the global markets, what do you feel will be the impact on China? What should we do now to prepare for this? What would you do? I'd be interested in your comments. Lots of people have views here and the more we take on your thinking the better off we will be. The economists predict 8-9% growth for China's economy next year. Do you think you can grow faster or slower than the market? That is where the challenge and opportunity is in managing the business. I certainly hope we can grow faster than 9% as everyone expects this to be the case for themselves. Please be prepared for a fun and interesting year next year... and let's be prepared to beat the market.

Environmental Tip of the Week

Artificial lighting accounts for 44% of the electricity use in office buildings. Please make it a habit to turn off the lights when you're leaving any room for 15 minutes or more and utilize natural light when you can.

****

Monday Morning Mail

Keep digital recordings of all client interviews, October 6, 2008

I hope those of you who had time for a break and for some rest are feeling recharged. We will need this as we go into the last quarter of this year. I hope you took some time to be with family, friends and those nearest and dearest to you. Let Q4 begin!

One lesson of the week... came from our Investor Relations team and the importance of recording every interview your clients conduct. Read below:

> "Today, we learned the value of keeping a digital recording of all interviews. We had a client who was misquoted and we were able to send the digital recording and transcript and get it fixed (at least they've said they are going to fix it). Without the recording, there would have been no way to prove that case. Lesson learned today... keep the digital recording filed away until the article comes out and the client has read the article."

We also faced a number of crises and issues that have evolved from the Internet and bloggers. I cannot express enough the importance of monitoring the blogs for coverage of your clients. I believe we do this well with most clients, but we need to get in the habit of treating this medium like we treat all others. We also need to do the influence audit for those bloggers covering our client issues often. If you don't know who writes about your clients most often online, I suggest you take time to study this.

Environmental Tip of the Week

For many of you in China, the TRC passed along recyclable shopping bags for us to use when shopping in the future. Why not open this and use it in the coming months... or, if you don't have this, limit any type of bag a vendor tries to offer you. Every little bit counts..

****

Client Service

*Understanding audience groups and what messages resonate,
November 3, 2008*

Dear Friends,

For those of you who have not been tuning in, the US presidential election has provided the world with great entertainment, promise and worry over the past two years. I will refrain from sharing any personal views other than to say that I have never been more reassured about the value of our profession. The campaign teams of both candidates are managing the messages on a daily basis. They are led by public communications professionals who understand audience groups and what messages resonate and they are tweaking these on a daily basis. If you subscribe to the definition of the public relations professional, as described by the late Edward Bernays, considered the father of public relations, then you can see how important the public relations professional is. Edward Bernays defined public relations as follows: ***"a public relations professional is an applied social scientist who advises a client on the social attitudes and actions to take in order to win support of the publics upon whom his or her viability depends."*** I had a client once tell me the best PR people he had worked with were former political campaign managers, who understand the importance of the message and how it should be managed. I urge us all to think not only about the message, but also about the management of this during the lifetime of a campaign and the role research plays.

****

Exploit our network, size and scale, January 12, 2009

Dear Colleagues,

I am going to promise all of you now that the *Monday Morning Mail* in 2009 will not be a continuous rant about financial turmoil and pressures. This is a fact of the environment we are all going to have to live with. Your leaders are looking at ways to manage through this and thrive. What I hope each and every member of Ogilvy PR will do is to think how you can do more to secure our future. Do more for the company... and for your clients. We need to win a major share of new business we go after, preserve and grow our relationships with our current clients, and build upon our own culture and expertise. Personally I am optimistic, charged up and feeling hugely competitive now, and this comes from not knowing what the future holds, but knowing that there are pockets of opportunity that will pop up in the year to come. We need to be nimble and ready and, although I am the fattest I have ever been, I am feeling very nimble and ready right now.

It is clear to me that we have two MAJOR things going for us at this moment in time. And that is our "Network" and our "Size and Scale". And we must, must make this work for us. We need now, more than ever before, to demonstrate the added value that comes from the Ogilvy organization and we must dip into every corner of this organization to help our clients succeed. This takes a lot of teamwork, and I hope that everyone digs down deep to find ways to help and be generous with your time for us to meet our goal of being the most influential PR firm in China.

****

Combatting a crisis online, March 30, 2009

There is a lot of speculation about the expectations for the Chinese economy this year. Many predict an 8% growth rate, while others say it is more likely to be 5%. Either way, I remain optimistic about growth in China and our own prospects. We also have a few interesting leads from Chinese companies beginning to think about their global expansion. With our global network we are really very well placed to handle such assignments and this is very encouraging.

This Week in Digital

Here are thoughts about combatting a crisis online:

- *Engage your influencers. There is no better case for knowing who the online influencers are and having an established relationship with them. We are developing our own influencer management database to ensure we never forget a birthday, milestone or the occasional dinner or event invite. We can really turn to them in good times and bad.*

- *Please note that in China all our competitors pay blogs in good times and bad. We seek to differentiate by championing new media relationships, not cash payments.*

- Keyword advertising is a great way to get your message in the forums where the conversation is taking place (and not where people are oblivious to it). Ditto buying search keywords from Baidu.

- In some cases directly responding to negative comments can be a good thing, if only to direct them to a crisis minisite.

- Monitoring is good to measure sentiment, volume, etc.

> Environmental Tip of the Week
>
> I hope you turned off your lights Saturday night! If not, why not do it tonight?

****

Be wary of overcommitting if you can't deliver, June 7, 2010

Good morning friends,

While I love the rush of new business, we must also be highly conscious that our quality does not suffer. It is better to say "no" and pass something up than to commit to something that we cannot deliver. We also need to strengthen our craft around our clients' campaigns. Does the work we are doing have strong ideas behind them? How are we bringing this to life daily? As counselors and leaders, these are the questions you should be asking yourself. Finally, a word about finishing 2010; while Debby and I have confidence about this year, we are not without our challenges. We need a combination of farming existing client opportunities and a few new client assignments to meet our commitments. We are confident we can do this, but it will take getting the work right, honing our ideas, and digging deeper into what is happening in China and translating this into ideas for our clients.

****

Monday Morning Mail

Rather do less better than deliver more average work, June 21, 2010

One thing about cases is that they are a demonstration of our work. And that is my present obsession. I have received a few notes of late from clients that like our ideas and believe we can do the work, but they have concerns about the quality of the product we are delivering. This is showing its signs in slowing payments, renegotiating of fees and having to do some tasks multiple times. We must tighten ourselves up and I am hoping each Director immerses themselves in the work to ensure we are delivering a product we would all be proud of. I would rather do less better than do more and deliver average work. So please everyone's attention to the details is a must.

****

Defend budgets by changing conversation from 'cost' to 'value', July 19, 2010

Dear Friends,

The one topic occupying my mind this week is "MONEY"; How we make money and how we talk about money. This topic is on my mind because I was told on Friday that we lost a client because they said our budgets were 2x that of the competition. Last week we also received many requests for proposals with no budget framework attached. Their request: "tell us how much we need to spend."

On the first topic, this is not new. Most of our clients complain we are expensive. For some, anything over $1 would be expensive. What is important we do in such circumstances is to change the discussion to "value." It is not about how much something costs, but rather the value of the services provided. If we can help resolve a potential million dollar crisis for US$100,000, that is value. So my advice here as we construct and defend budgets is that we must be prepared to defend our budgets by changing the conversation from "Cost" to "Value", and we also need to know what the client defines as value. Then, we must deliver this like no one else can! When someone goes out and buys a LV bag and spends US$5,000 it is because it is valuable, not because it costs that much. Same is true for us.

On the second topic, I get increasingly worried about requests for proposals that don't define the budgets they are willing to spend. I worry here because it is a sign that the client is just fishing around and he/she has not really thought about their brief. So please be careful here. You need to find the parameters of what they are willing to spend. Questions like: "should we focus on recommendations in the US$100,000 range... or something a bit more ambitious like US$200-400,000?" It is true that sometimes clients really don't know how much public relations services cost and we need to give them a budget, but we risk wasting a lot of time on proposals if we don't home in on what they are willing to spend early on. Giving them ideas of what others spend for getting xyz is helpful. Note also, if a potential client has worked in PR before and they ask, "what are you willing to do this for," you must be careful.

I share these two points with you because our time is extremely valuable and there just isn't enough time for us in the day, week, month, year. So getting the money discussion right early I hope will help us all in our new business proposal process.

> ### Environmental Tip of the Week
>
> One thing that has amazed me about Taiwan after living here for four years in the early 1990s is the transformation the Island has made in the area of the environment. When I moved here in 1991 everyone complained about the environment. It was a constant topic of conversation... just like what is happening in Beijing now. But after 15 years, I don't hear much about pollution anymore. In Taipei there is a very aggressive, active recycling campaign that has taken place that everyone follows. It is much more sophisticated and successful than anywhere I have travelled and it makes me believe that such campaigns are possible. Ask the Taiwan colleagues in each of your offices to tell you more about this.

On a final note, I want to commend the offices in Taiwan for their discipline in starting meetings on time and sticking to allotted time frames for such meetings. In both offices meetings were run efficiently and effectively and when there was an agreement to begin at 5:00pm, everyone was in the room by 5:00pm at Era Ogilvy PR. Same is true at Ogilvy PR. Everyone showed up at 10:00am sharp. We need to learn from such discipline, at least in our China operations.

****

Monday Morning Mail

PR exec arrested for running smear campaign, October 25, 2010

Dear Friends,

We're doing well with the momentum going into year-end. In the public relations business, being busy is good. The gold standard in this business is to be paid and respected for our strategic counsel as well as the execution of our ideas, and I can feel this coming through with many campaigns... so thank you. We are far from being perfect and there is a lot of work to do across the board, but some of the campaigns we are running - Goodyear, Chengdu Pambassadors, IBM, Intel and Pfizer to name a few - are influential in the China market and they are being talked about, and I am delighted we are part of this.

This week also saw a local PR practitioner allegedly hired by Meng Niu arrested for running a smear campaign against Yili. While all of the facts are not clear, this case put the PR industry in the spotlight in China. Since well before I began in this business the public relations industry has had its own image problem. People often refer to the PR business as spin, tweaking facts here and there and often dealing in half-truths. I want you to know that I am strongly against any type of "negative campaigning" at all. We just do not and will not do this, and if asked, we should refuse. That's not the way we do business. We work to build brands based on their benefits and competitive strengths, not on rumor-mongering and the like. I hope all of us can build a PR business in North Asia that is truly respected for dealing in facts and honesty, and in my opinion there is no better public relations campaign for a company than dealing with truth. Please consider this in everything we do and feel free to write me with questions or comments if you have them.

****

Analyze cool campaigns to find out how and why they work, May 23, 2011

Dear Friends:

A few questions to begin today's *Monday Morning Mail*. When someone asks you what you do, how do you articulate this? When someone asks you what was the insight behind a campaign, what do you say? Or, how was the insight turned into an idea? Or, how was the idea executed and what was the result? Can you quantify the result with specific metrics? How simple do we make this?

These questions have obsessed me of late. I know very few people who do this really well in our business. Yet, saying something is "cool" without giving it some type of strategic framework for me personally speaks of laziness. I believe we must get into the practice of explaining the context of an idea very simply, what was an insight that led to an idea and how was the idea executed with metrics associated. Take the "women car driver's viral" from Shanghai for example. This is a brilliant execution. The context: women drivers are on the rise, no tire company is speaking to them or see them as a potential customer. Women are not interested in normal topics related to tires. The goal: To build brand awareness and get women excited about our client's tires' "safety" differentiator. The insight: women are largely interested in topics related to women, and lately the topic of finding "Mr. Right" is very popular. The idea: dramatize, exaggerate and entertain women customers by getting them to chat online about tires. Do this by getting them to compare a good tire to a good man! The execution: Create a 15-second viral video with two women talking about what appears to be a man, but is really a tire of client's brand. Promote it through multiple channels. The result: Brand awareness grew from 12% to 16% in the period the campaign ran. 1.8 million people visited the site. Over 17,000 comments about the campaign. Good tire "man" becomes a hot topic among women.

It is easy to say, "watch this cool" viral, but the real marketing professional in my view will think a bit deeper and work to articulate why something is what it is. I for one am becoming a student of campaigns. What is the message? Why? How is it presented? Executed? What was the business result? Each question should have a simple answer, but it really requires some thinking.

My wish for us all is that we all can do this... become "idea nerds" and that we can really intelligently talk about an idea with some strategic framework other than, "hey dude, this is cool."

****

Ask yourself a few strategic questions, June 7, 2011

Dear Friends,

All in all we are doing well for the year. We do have some challenges, however, as the world turns and many of our traditionally large clients are struggling with their leadership. We also have more and better competition around the region that has beat us in some pitches of late.

As we approach mid-year it is a good time to take stock of where we are and where we are headed and to ask ourselves a few very strategic questions.

- Is everything we do contributing to the bottom line of our client companies?
- Are we running exciting, engaging and industry leading campaigns that have a strong idea at the center?
- Are we executing flawlessly?
- What more can we do to delight our clients?
- Are we earning our fees and then some?

Please think about these questions, and then think about your own behavior, discipline and performances. I find that the people who are working well with their clients and doing great work are often those that love what they are doing. And the people coming to work day-to-day and dreading what they do are frequently being challenged. What this tells me as a manager is to find assignments our teams love and deliver above and beyond on these, and to correct those situations where we are struggling. It is the only way to get ahead in my view.

****

How 'intelligent' is our 'market intelligence'?, August 15, 2011

Dear Friends,

This week my mind has been occupied with the concept of "market intelligence" and wondering how truly "intelligent" we are as an organization. I sat in two meetings last week where the Managing Directors of two different client organizations asked me specifically what I felt about xyz article written about the company in a specific publication. I was amazed they read the translations of the articles we gave them so closely and further surprised that, as a habit, they read our media clipping reports first thing every morning when they arrive in the office. I then went to the teams to ask them if they read these articles and they looked at me in amazement. My week finished off by a client asking about the hours we spend on "market intelligence" and the client asked me "how intelligent" is this really and how is it being applied by your teams? All very good questions.

Some of the very early definitions of a PR person by none other than the father of public relations, Edward Bernays, defined PR in this way:

> "...by my definition, a public relations person is an applied social scientist who advises a client or employer on the social attitudes and actions to take in order to win support of the publics upon whom his or her or its viability depends."

The ability to be an applied social scientist - one definition for PR - comes first and foremost to a deep understanding of the environment, what is being said, by who, when, where and more. We must understand this before the client does so that we can inform, advise and guide them appropriately. We need to be intelligent!

To me, what this means is that we need to think through our practices and behaviors and to do a reality check to determine how intelligent we really are in managing our clients. These conversations were a wake-up call for me and I hope they will get you thinking about what might change in the way you counsel your clients.

****

Reinforcing a reputation for superior service, August 30, 2011

Dear Colleagues,

On Wednesday night of last week I had the pleasure of dining with Debby Cheung in Shanghai. We were talking about the future of our business and the twists and turns our industry has taken and could take. We talked about a restaurant in China whose reputation was built from its overwhelming superior service. One couple who asked to take away the watermelon served for desert was given a real watermelon to ensure the customers could keep this very fresh instead of eating the pre-cut fruit which would spoil quickly. The customers wrote about this on weibo (their microblog) and the rest was history. The restaurant's reputation of a superior service provider was reinforced... all by word of mouth.

It made me think when was the last time you did that for your client? When did we send along three extra ideas, along with the monthly status report of what we are doing for our clients? How often are we trying to explain to our clients they must pay us more for some type of service, without first thinking how much real value this created for the company. The "happiness chemicals" began to filter in. I thought about the possibilities of what could be. I started to think about our current clients and then our possible new business. I think this is something that we should keep in mind and exercise in greater ways throughout our North Asia business.

I also conducted a few interviews with potential candidates. I was surprised that one came 30 minutes late. The other two showed up wearing no suit, no tie, and they were much too casual for my comfort level. Is this where the world is headed? I know that dress and client expectations are changing, but I do not want Ogilvy to lead the way in loosening up of some disciplines that speak of professionalism to our clients. That means we must continue to dress the part and deliver the high-quality recommendations, in a clean and professional way.

One thing I like to do is have a dialogue with senior clients. In casual discussions I can find out what is bothering them, what more we can do, and I can hear about the good things you are all doing. These senior clients will also call me when something is not just right. I had two calls like that last week and I feel blessed to have these relationships so that we can get out in front of problems instead of them sneaking up on us. Please DO NOT underestimate the power of a regular check-in with your key clients to check the temperature of whether what we are doing for them is truly delivering value.

****

Do not forget our core competence, December 19, 2011

Are you having fun? I hope you will take some time to think about this question. I have found that the people in our business who are having fun, understand the broader role they are playing and have good client relationships consistently perform better than those who question whether the PR business is right for them. Certainly not every moment is pure "fun", but I certainly hope the balance of enjoyable tasks and requests outpace those that are tedious and painful. As I travelled the US last week (New York and San Francisco), I had a chance to catch up with many colleagues and friends. Most are having fun and performing exceptionally well. Those folks "down in the dumps" I encouraged to find their happiness or do themselves a favor and move on.

As a firm we are having a very good year. In North Asia we are doing our share. All of our markets are having strong years and our opportunities are immense. Anytime I wake up in the morning and see 3-5 new business opportunities in my email, I know we are doing something very right. As usual, my antennae also tell me there are many places we must improve and the competition is getting better, but I certainly feel we can compete and win at the highest level in all of our markets, and as your designated leader, this is most encouraging. So thank you for all you do, and for also being anxious about how we can improve ourselves bit by bit. We are in the planning season now and like all successful businesses we need to identify where our growth areas are going to come from, and I hope everyone feels they have a role in this. As you read this I am sitting with a number of your leaders and colleagues discussing the next five years in China. Please do not be shy to share your own views of what you think the next five years should look like for this company and the role you would like to play. I hope one goal for everyone is to "have more fun."

****

More 'vision' skill, less 'strategery', December 5, 2011

Dear All,

Strategery and Vision. These are the two themes I will dive into in this week's *Monday Morning Mail*.

Strategery, according to our client David Petrou, Global Head of Communications for Jones Day, is the act of a bunch of people sitting around in a room and talking about "strategic things", thinking they are smart without anything ever really getting done. He used this in response to a description I gave of one staff member's "strategic" strength on his business. He said, "Scott, globally we have a lot of folks giving us 'strategic recommendations', but not enough who are actually executing. I call that 'strategery.' I prefer smart people to work on my business who get stuff done, no matter what it takes." Strategy without passion, a strong client focus or an ability to execute does not interest me, he said. I believe that this is true for all clients so, please, when you begin to consider all sorts of "strategic" thoughts, ask yourself if your clients know how much you care and have confidence in your abilities. To me, this will make any strategic recommendation much more powerful.

Vision is the second theme of focus this week. This is not the vision we expect from our leaders, or our client CEOs in running their businesses. It is the "account management vision" to "see how one decision or action will impact another down the line". I remember one star staffer of H-Line Ogilvy coming to me in November when she learned she was pregnant, discussing with me how to manage an account for the next nine months as her client's contract would be up for renewal when she would be away delivering her child. That to me is great account management vision. This "vision" skill is very important for all of us in public relations.

****

Do not forgot our core competence, December 19, 2011

Dear Friends,

In what was a milestone event for Ogilvy PR and for China, 16 global and China representatives of Ogilvy PR spent Sunday through Thursday in Chengdu presenting ideas for the next phase of our Branding Chengdu work. Throughout the course of the week we were entertained by the Mayor, visited the industrial park and museum, hugged Pandas, ate more Sichuan food than you can imagine, debated great ideas and talked about the future of the PA Practice, headed by Jamie Moeller, Ogilvy PR's Public Affairs Global Managing Director.

Although in the last *Monday Morning Mail* I warned us against pontificating too much about "strategic this" and "strategic that", this week I do want to highlight the importance of "strategy" in everything we do. At times I worry that we are putting forward plans and recommendations that are heavy on execution without reinforcing the core messages we believe are important to our client campaigns. And these plans are being submitted without an explanation of the basic rationale for developing those messages. These are not messages that clients feed us, but they are the ones that we glean from knowing our client's customers better than anyone and showing that we have a differentiated and deeper point of view. Please, when you are making a recommendation, do not forget that our core competence is helping our clients communicate more effectively, and such competence begins with deep, differentiated understanding of our client's business, the world they are communicating in, and the messages that differentiate them and help them achieve a certain result. Such strategic underpinning of our campaigns is essential to our offering.

Client Service

Much new business is won or lost at budget stage, October 8, 2012

Dear Friends,

Money! This is a topic that many people do not like talking about in our business, but is something that is essential. In my view everyone working at Ogilvy PR is entitled to a fair and decent salary which should be commensurate with your contribution to the company. At the management level, to pay fair and decent salaries we need to drive revenue into the company. And personally I hope everyone is happy with their salaries, but not too happy as I love for us to be ambitious for ourselves, for our clients and for Ogilvy PR. But this is not a note about your personal compensation.

I am writing about money as it relates to charging clients for our work product. By properly charging clients we can drive the revenue to allow us the room to grow professionally, personally and financially. I am reminded of this because during this October break we have been brought into many situations whereby we have been asked for help, but with no mention of $$. In one case a client asked for a ton of research to be done on a pro-bono basis. This is not a non-profit organization and I politely declined but offered to do the research for a small fee. We now have 5,000 pounds to support the work of a planner to do some basic research. In another case Jeremy Webb and I were brought into a crisis case during the holiday. Before we got too deep into the engagement, we sent a two-page memo outlining our approach and our fees for covering a few weeks of service.

The reason I am covering this topic in the *Monday Morning Mail* is to impress upon all of us the importance of asking for "budget parameters" early on in the client engagement. While we do not want to be perceived as money hungry, or just interested in "the budget," we do need the discipline to uncover what type of budgets a client has for the work they expect us to undertake. Too often clients are fishing around agencies for ideas and I worry that we spend a lot of time cultivating a client without the knowledge of whether or not he or she has the proper resources to support our efforts. What we need to do is find a way to tactfully ask, "campaigns of this type usually run xyz in fees, does that represent the type of resources you have for this effort?" In my 27 years I have found that clients that have defined a budget to support a campaign are much more serious than those that do not offer budget guidelines. And while I would not want us to turn away an opportunity from a client who is fishing for budget parameters, I urge caution in proceeding if we don't have an idea of the resources they have set aside for the support they are requesting.

This is a topic that I could write much more on, but I want us to use sensitivity, discipline and discretion, as so many new business assignments and engagements are won and lost at the budget stage and we could serve ourselves much better by getting this right early.

****

The impact of 'big data' on our business, November 26, 2012

This past week Americans throughout the world celebrated Thanksgiving. Without getting into technicalities, this is a holiday whereby we give thanks for everything we have in our lives. So in the spirit of this holiday I would like to thank all of you for your contributions to Ogilvy PR this year and in the past. We have such a dream business and I am thankful for this everyday. I am also convinced our #1 competitor is not another PR firm. Our challenge is realizing the possibilities ahead of us. I am just back from a trip to New York and I have never felt better about our opportunities, but it is going to take discipline, work and commitment getting there and I have no doubt we are up for the challenge.

What is top of mind with me is the topic of "Big Data" and how it is going to impact our business. I read an article on how the Obama Administration used big data to win the election and I never felt more excited, because this targeting was all about what we do in PR. But I also felt anxious. Anxious because this area of data mining and analysis is somewhat new to us people who delve in the "ideas and words" business. Rest assured you will see movements we make in leveraging data to help us target better and this will be one of my focus areas in the year to come. I also saw a presentation from a person who runs a PR firm in the US whose positioning is "Data Mining To Drive Decisions." The reality is that CEOs and CMOs of this world are interested in "Big Ideas" but to get their attention they need to be embedded in persuasive numbers presentations.

****

Client Service

Honesty and specificity with clients, two-way dialogue with consumers, June 17, 2013

My serotonin levels were unusually high at the end of last week thanks to a four-way pitch where Ogilvy PR is looking to be the winner. There was other good news coming in throughout the network as well that comforted me in knowing we are doing well. The particular assignment I just mentioned is a whole new area for us and the client entrusted us above their global agency and global financial advisor to be their partner in China. New engagements in new areas that stretch us as a firm is the way to grow in this business and I am feeling good about this new chance at a growth spurt.

HONESTY and SPECIFICITY are two other words that come to mind when thinking about the learnings of this pitch and the previous win we just had. In terms of HONESTY, in both circumstances we were asked tough questions about the government process and likelihood. In both cases, we answered honestly... not with what they wanted to hear, but with what we thought was the best characteristic of the situation in China. They appreciated this. The second learning was that in both cases we were very specific. Very specific and it was clear we knew what we were talking about. Broad brush strokes at "a menu of what you can do" does not win new business.

Other learnings/lessons this week: last weekend I spent three days at the FORTUNE Global Forum in Chengdu, a huge gathering of CEOs in which we managed press efforts for the Chengdu government. In one of the sessions I heard Muthar Kent, CEO of Coca-Cola say "the biggest change in our business has come from the consumer in the way they consume information. Today it is all about 'two-way' dialogue." Welcome Social@! This is not new, but with Mr. Kent expressing this I feel that this is significant. Second theme was everything related to mobile and how tablets, phones, etc. are now serving as new media platforms. The third theme was all about urbanization and smarter cities. Alert Branding States! I found the Forum most interesting in terms of content and among the best conferences I have attended.

****

Monday Morning Mail

Don't shrink from tackling difficult subjects, July 29, 2013

Dear Friends,

I am wrapping up my travels this week and am looking forward to my return on August 7. We are in an "always on", 24 hours, seven days of the week business. When our clients are facing difficulties or need something, they need us to be connected and responsive and staffed to address their needs. I am most grateful to those folks who have covered for me in my absence this past month, and I have also enjoyed staying close to the many developments that have transpired. My hope for you and us is that you also have time to take a breather, but you find a way to stay connected and covered if the need arises. Fortunately for us and for our clients the wheels of commerce in North Asia continue to spin.

For us in North Asia this month has served up many opportunities. It seems like client issues and crisis situations have been percolating in China and fortunately we are the point of contact for many current and emerging crisis situations. This dynamic reinforces my belief that truly great public relations firms are connected in various ways to the markets in which they operate. Our leads have come from previous clients, law firms, investment banks and our best source of referrals is from existing clients. So thank you to everyone who plugs away at networking and being connected to drive our business forward.

The one message I would like to send to all of you today relates to the way we "talk about our business", and the confidence we have in "talking about difficult subjects" like conflicts and billing. On the "talking about our business" subject, my belief is that we must find every chance we can to talk about what we do. If you find yourself talking about media monitoring or press releases or press conferences you are missing the bigger picture. These are tactics that we use to help our clients achieve larger business goals that require professional branding or communications. One reason why we are asking every office and practice group to develop award cases are to help us articulate more strategically the work we do. On "talking about difficult subjects" we must practice and learn how to ask for the order. How to tell our clients that "for these services our fees are xx$." We need to look our clients in the eyes and with confidence explain that those are the fees that we will charge for the time of you and your teams. We are in the service business and time is how we make money. We must work smartly and efficiently and also ensure we charge a reasonable and fair price for the time you will spend. This money discussion is often clumsy for people who don't believe their time is worth what they charge, and that is a big problem. It is a confidence issue and we must be confident in our recommendations and prepared to charge our clients for our time. Also on the topic of difficult subjects, talking about how to manage conflicts is imperative. We are in a big and successful network and our success often presents a number of conflict assignments. We have been able to manage these because of our honesty and transparency and we cannot delay or avoid speaking about these topics with our clients. Over the past few weeks I have seen a number of problems arise from clumsiness in how we talk about our business and I hope we can all improve upon this in the months to come.

****

Don't shy away from areas of 'discomfort', October 14, 2013

The topic of this week's *Monday Morning Mail* is "discomfort" and how important I believe it is to our future development as a professional services firm. I am presently deeply involved in two client cases. One is a branding assignment for a client that has a very complicated structure in a highly challenged industry. The client hired us to help them define their brand at the corporate level to give them added punch in the China market. They have invested a lot in China and they have much to offer. They certainly need a corporate brand. What makes this difficult is that they know they need a stronger brand to compete in the market, but they don't really know where this assignment is headed. When we ask them what they need it makes them uncomfortable because they don't know. What we do know is that once we define the brand it will not be used to create a TVC. Yet, the field is open in terms of how and where this communication will be used in the future. I have observed us in meetings probing the client to find out what they want and it is obvious they don't know. This whole process has been very interesting to me and has also made me uncomfortable. We are doing Big Ideal workshops, Fusion planning and brand consulting all wrapped up into one assignment. The client told me that this is the first time anywhere globally the company has reached outside for help in this area. The stakes are high and I have felt discomfort for the past month regarding anything related to this client. One thing I know, however, is that I can feel myself growing professionally through this process.

The second client is another where the stakes are high. It involves a major crisis and a possible fine. The client hired us to help them communicate their offering and significance to the China market and to minimize their fine. Again, this assignment has brought us into areas we have not been before. Our counsel is very strong and we are doing well. I have been "on the edge" though because it is all relatively new to us. It is fascinating and exciting and a constant source of discomfort. What is great is that I feel I am learning and it is also stretching us in ways we have not been before.

What is my message?: I think we all have to look for areas that make us uncomfortable and to not shy away but rather embrace them. How uncomfortable are you?

****

Client love and deep roots, March 17, 2014

Two topics for this week's *Monday Morning Mail*. The first is about "Client Love." The second is about "Deep Roots." Let me explain.

Client Love. It is no surprise that the teams and offices who handle clients they love are highly successful. In some special concoction of client service provided by our teams, clients who are the recipients of love get the best ideas and the most passionate support. Conversely, the relationships I see in the network that are very transactional and further complicated by difficult clients (or the wrong chemistry on our side) rarely survive. I have been part of many conversations recently with both clients who love us and clients who are thinking of leaving us. I get a rush of optimism from those that value us. And, I am troubled by those where our relationships are on ice. So with this note I am begging you to evaluate your client love. Which bucket do you fall into? Will you go to great lengths to deliver superior results? Or, do you get an uneasy feeling when you have to engage? If you are in the former group, congratulations. If you are in the latter, this needs addressing or it will most certainly end unfavorably. We are working hard to try to close our back door. Back door meaning the clients who we have had but have left us or are planning to do so. I believe if we get the client love component right we will be well on our way to success.

Deep Roots. As I travel office-to-office it is also telling that the most successful offices we have are deeply rooted into their local markets. In these offices if a client asks us who are the most influential people in a number of areas, we not only know the names, but we can connect the dots. Deeply-rooted offices are at the center of the big briefs coming out of the market, and we are on every RFP list. Deep Roots requires an investment in time, but this investment is a must for survival. In my opinion the most successful PR firms are those that are deeply rooted and it comes with the territory of our domain expertise. So as a second exercise I hope you will all think about our market connectivity and consider what few things you can do to strengthen our roots in your local market. Setting up advisory task forces, doing important pro-bono (or low-bono) work that puts you into a more influential network is part of this. We can discuss this more as we move on in the year, but I do want us thinking about our "rooting" in each market and work to strengthen this.

****

Eating humble pie and earning client respect in a crisis, March 31, 2014

Humble Pie! "To eat humble pie" is an expression in English that means "to face humiliation for a serious error." Well, Monday through Wednesday of this week I felt like I was eating humble pie for breakfast, lunch and dinner. We had a few setbacks that we absolutely must learn from. We are much better as a network and we cannot afford to get fat eating humble pie. The week started with client anxiety around a global thought leadership study we are promoting. For a variety of reasons the study wasn't getting the traction we needed in the US and UK, and we were being challenged about our global network capabilities. We are addressing this now. I also was told that an event we supported in China received "very low marks" despite glowing results. Finally, I had a call with an important regional client who is anxious because she is betting on Ogilvy PR for a huge campaign and she needs to make sure all of our ducks are in order. Needless to say I did a lot of apologizing and explaining this week. My ambition for us is to sell not by words, but by our actions, and while we will have peaks and dips in our relationships, we need to do everything possible to delight and deliver. I do not want the *Monday Morning Mail* to be a series of euphoric "we are great" notes. We had some slips this week and we are better than this. So here is the only way out of this I know:

"Get close to your clients. If you are speaking to them daily, you will not be surprised!" In the first example above, we were close at the center, but not at the spokes. We need to address that. In the second example, we were the co-ordinating body amongst many interested parties, however, we MUST make sure we know who the real client is before we assume responsibility. The third example is less extreme, but again, connectivity and responsibility at the spokes (beyond the center) is needed. Success is all about taking the time to connect. Emails won't do it all. We must get on the phone and connect and keep everyone informed. To me, this is basic account management that we must get right. So please, let's dot our "i's" and cross our "t's" and do the extra step to ensure no one is confused.

A story: In China this week we had a client in crisis. They called us to ask for help because they had an aggravated customer who was meeting with a store manager. The client was not in Beijing and they asked if we could go and support the store manager. The client leader asked me for support. She mentioned casually that "this was not in our scope" and should we do this? I answered quite curtly, "absolutely." These cases are inflection points in client relationships and no one cares about scope. We showed up. Supported the client. And won love in the process.

The lesson: If you are close to your client, they will respect your time. You won't have "scope" issues and I promise you these relationships will grow!

****

Surprise and delight in serving the client, April 28, 2014

What inspires you?

As storytellers we must find the ideas and touch points that inspire people. And who doesn't like to be inspired?

This whole topic of "inspiration" was sparked by a meeting I had with an old Ogilvy colleague recently. He was reflecting on his days at the agency and said he used to get the biggest rush by doing things for clients that were unexpected. Like sending a link to an interesting article, sharing an idea or campaign that shows great thinking, highlighting something that offered a differentiated view. The surprise and delight in serving the client! He was making this comment because as a client he didn't feel like he was getting this and wondered where the true partnership in client-agency relations has gone. I was inspired by this conversation and made a note to share it with all of you. I believe this is about "client love" and by doing some little things for our clients, they will be inspired by us, and in return this will have a multiplier impact for our relationships. What do you think? Why not try to do something out of the ordinary for your clients and see what happens?

****

Client Service

Order maker or order taker?, May 26, 2014

Are you an "order maker" or an "order taker"?

This challenge to our service was top of mind as I met with a number of clients this past two weeks. I heard comments such as:

- *"You do well off the brief, but can you surprise me sometimes?"*
- *"Your Director just repeats the brief to me, acknowledging she understands but does not come back with any point of view."*
- *"Please do not come in and do a credentials presentation. Everyone does credentials. Come in with ideas and some thoughts on how you can build my business."*
- *"We can do most of what you do in-house. What you need to do is find our gaps and provide solutions to fill those gaps."*
- *"You don't understand our business enough. Can you deploy staff to sit with us and I promise you more business will come your way."*

Let's remember that at the core of what we do is develop marketing/communications ideas that solve business problems. Order makers embrace client problems and surprise them with ideas that they cannot do themselves. Ideas that are valued and demand the type of fees we charge. Order takers respond to requests with little or no added value.

One thing I am certain about is the marketplace for order takers is limited. We might as well work in a restaurant where order taking comes with a nominal value. Order makers create opportunities and that is where I believe all of us should focus.

As an entire organization we need to be clear that our clients are our lifeline. Without clients, no Ogilvy. We have to love our clients. Build their businesses. Commit to them. We need to recognize that all client relationships are not perfect and we need to address them if they are not. We need to be prepared to spend our work lives together with our clients and become part of their organization. By doing so, we will become much more valuable and informed. And if we don't, I don't even want to think about the ramifications.

****

Monday Morning Mail

The need to leverage our entire arsenal, July 28, 2014

The *Monday Morning Mail* is back! I took a brief hiatus from sending this while I travelled through the US evaluating universities with my daughter and family. We visited eight universities and it was very interesting to hear how they pitched themselves. There were many, many similarities. After the eight visits, I reflected on which university stood out in how they pitched themselves. Two were outstanding. From the lecture to the tour they touched a personal cord. They cut through. It made me think a lot about our own pitches and the process clients go through in selecting a communications partner. For me, the gold standard is to strive to be the agency clients desire to work with. The Harvard or the Oxford of the professional service firms. When we get to that level, we won't have to pitch. It will be a discussion and a selection. I would love us to get to that level, but we are far away from that today. However, I certainly hope that we are the most creative and effective partners for our clients, and I hope they feel a real difference in working with us.

I was reminded of this on Friday in a discussion with a big client win in Beijing. At the moment this client must remain confidential, but after a review of eight agencies we were selected. They loved our idea, appreciated most of the team and they felt a real difference. They met with me to send a message: they care about the execution. I assured them we would be an agency of a different nature. One that they would see a marked difference in our service vs. others. I was very proud of the team who won this, and now the proof is in the pudding. The questions I want to ask each of us at Ogilvy PR are these: what type of engagement experience are we giving our clients? Is it the very best the market has to offer? Is it different and full of care, concern and creativity? Is it delivering the goods? We are seeing the competition get better across our markets and we continually need to raise the bar in what we are offering.

The above brings me to my next point about something concrete that makes us different and that is our network, and the oil that makes our network thrive is the concept of teamwork.

How to win in the new competitive era we face in Asia? I believe one way to do so is to leverage the totality of what the Ogilvy network has to offer. Our knowledge management team led by Karen Ooi and Betsy Hui are working to make sure our regional expertise is available at everyone's fingertips. We have technology solutions in the works that will be launched shortly that will help us connect even more with informed expertise. We have communities of practices and initiatives. We have the Ogilvy Brains community that brings people in Asia together to discuss new business and the sharing of ideas around the new business. There are a lot of very smart people within the Ogilvy Group and our global network. We need to break down the borders and connect, connect, connect. To me, in the best interests of our clients and the development of our people, we need to make the most of Ogilvy to work towards their success. That means tapping people with skills from different disciplines and different markets. It takes initiative, however, and a mindset that there is someone out there in the Ogilvy world doing something that may be valuable to our clients. We need to tap that. I believe that is what we must do, and we need to leverage our entire arsenal. If you are looking for someone with a specific expertise, start by surfing our Intranet and if you don't find what you are looking for please ask Karen, Betsy or me.

****

Professionalism starts with the small details, August 25, 2014

The theme of today's *Monday Morning Mail* is all about "Professionalism." This is one of those topics that everyone has a definition for, and professionalism crosses all aspects of our business. I figured I would share a few observations I had this week in what I believe is professionalism, and also reflect on what I think it is going to take for us to continue our success in the future.

The first person I want to call out in this *Monday Morning Mail* is Amy Chan. Amy works in the Consumer team in Hong Kong and I was with this team over the weekend when they handled the Macau event for the Ultimate Fighting Championship (UFC). Amy was working the microphones during the press conference and as she walked around the room various journalists were asking questions. The journalists from China, who were relatively new to the UFC, asked a number of questions to the CEO in 'chinglish'. Dana White, the CEO, who is a larger than life character and very aggressive, couldn't understand the questions. He kept asking for clarification. Amy serving as both "deliverer of the microphone" and "interpreter" restated the question so he could understand. She handled this so brilliantly and so confidently, reflecting her knowledge of the sport and the fighters, that I sat in the press conference grinning. Huge call-out for Amy. Thank you. You made us proud and I was so impressed with your maturity and posture. To me, for this role in particular, that is demonstrating our professionalism.

Thirty-six hours earlier I was in a UPS meeting in the Hong Kong office. We spent the morning with UPS in a very informative client session. I was delighted to see Wing Fung, an Account Coordinator in the Corporate Team, recognize the clients' "water glasses" were empty. Wing proceeded to stand up, refill the water jug and serve the clients. Some people in this business think they are too senior to serve a client a drink, or to go out of their way to provide a service that does not relate directly to the client's brief we are trying to solve. I would like us all to remember that we are in the service business. Certainly we need to deliver creative and effective solutions for our clients, but before they are receptive to those ideas, they need to know we love and care about them, and that we are not too senior to serve them! Many people may disagree with me here, but I must tell you that for as long as I have been in this business, providing services of common courtesy are core to an overall professional approach. Serving water and coffee are the jobs of the tea and coffee personnel we have in the office, but when they are not there the youngest person in the team should pop up to show they know this is an important role for them. This service has largely been forgotten, but I am calling out Wing Fung because she demonstrated faith in that some people still recognize this importance. "Clients do not care how much you know, until they know how much you care." Let's not forget the importance of such traditions. Thank you Wing Fung for the reminder. Is that professionalism? It doesn't take a lot to serve a client water, but I would argue it is part of a total client experience and professionalism starts with the small details.

In the spirit of professionalism I have heard a number of minor complaints lately about our service and our product. These are small nicks and not stuff we will be fired for, but the complaints are certainly building on behalf of clients. These range from speed of delivery and making deadlines, to knowledge of our client's business, to questions we are asking to figure out a brief, to something I heard a lot recently... "Scott, can your team just give me something perfect that I can send along to my management without having to spend a half day changing it?" These comments reflect the evolving nature of our business. Clients want things fast. There is no time anymore for delays. If we are going to compete, we have to be more central to our client's organization as opposed to an outside vendor. The clients where our people are embedded are the ones that grow, and contact and review meetings once per month is not going to do it. The days of the great brief with detailed background provided by clients are gone. We need to be "order makers, not order takers." In today's world we must create the briefs for our clients and mine the insights. And finally, we need to get the stuff we do right the first time, on deadline, so our clients can review and send this to their constituencies. That is what is being asked of us, and this is part of the new professionalism we are being asked to deliver. In the past Ogilvy PR teams have been great at reflecting these changes and showing our clients we are different from others in everything we do. I believe we can embrace these requests and continually evolve our service, and I hope you agree with me.

****

Client Service

Back to basics, November 3, 2014

"Back to the basics" is the message for this week's *Monday Morning Mail*. As we begin to close the books on 2014 (only two months to go), there are a number of things at play within our network. You will see the leadership of our offices throughout the region working with all of you to meet and exceed the strategic and financial commitments we made throughout the year. Please support them! You will also see your leadership preparing for what I hope is a fantastic year in 2015. We began the year asking everyone to think about how we can be more proactive in everything we do, not waiting for a client to call, and working to be order makers vs. order takers. With our industry in a state of change getting the mix right between "order making" and "order taking" is extremely important. We have had a good year of winning new business and farming additional work from our existing clients and that is the lifeblood of our business. We need to celebrate such wins and recognize growing our client relationships gives us the means to take care of our people and invest for the future.

However, as we experience this change, we must take stock and we cannot forget the basics of how we have built our business. As our business has grown some of the basics of account management and service have faltered. This begins with being quick to respond to client requests. In many offices and client engagements, the meeting report or conference report has vanished. People respond on email and Wechat and there is no proper written communication with who is doing what by when. I have been told deadlines are getting missed, and while our work is creative and good, some of our competition are more disciplined in their day-to-day account management. The problems exist mostly with our retainer agreements. The blanket monthly fees for nondescript hours of client service are dangerous. What comes with these engagements are tons of expectations with challenges if we are not delivering value every minute. Finally, in a lot of the formal client meetings we have had, I find our staff do not wear formal business attire anymore. In some meetings, despite all of our clients wearing ties or formal business suits for women, we are much too casual. And don't get me started on the use of mobile phones for texting or even taking calls in the middle of client meetings. Last year we lost a pitch because a client felt we were disrespectful. Despite this being more of the norm today, this behavior is not acceptable in client meetings.

This note is a call out for everyone to remind us that we must get back to the fundamentals. No formal communication with a client should be sent without at least two people reviewing this. New staffers should not be left to their own devices in defining how they communicate with clients. They should be led and taught the Ogilvy way and it is the responsibility of their supervisors to make sure such mistakes are not made. This last week in a number of instances clients reached out to complain to me. Nothing to fire us about, but expectations of us that we in some way have not met. Whenever we are moving too fast and working around the clock, we need to take stock. No matter how fast we go we need to fix the sloppiness. If there is a problem with a client, don't email them. Get in front of them and iron out the problems. They hold the keys to our future. If for some reason a relationship is not working out, let your supervisor know. We need to be proactive in making sure our relationships are right. Sloppiness is not acceptable. In fact, when I began at Ogilvy I was told a typo in a client communication was a fireable offence. We must make sure we get the fundamentals right if we want to continue the success we have had.

****

Big Picture

Keeping a view on what is important — the Big Picture — is one ingredient for success.

Chapter Six

Big Picture

Opportunities in the wake of the banking crisis, October 13, 2008

Dear Colleagues,

This last week/month we witnessed something that I believe will become a historic milestone for us all. We are seeing a crisis in the banking world in the US that will impact the whole world and possibly life as we know it today.

Famous reputable financial brands like Bear Sterns, Lehman Brothers and Washington Mutual are names of the past. Merrill Lynch, Goldman Sachs and Morgan Stanley - financial powerhouses - have completely new business models and are structuring themselves for the future. Insurance firms the likes of AIG require significant government support to stay afloat.

And while many of us have not yet felt the effect of this meltdown, I believe it is around the corner. At least in the US, the basic message is that with the credit squeeze people are going to spend less. There will be fewer automobiles sold, fewer people taking vacations and travelling on business (affecting the airlines and hotels), fewer people eating out, fewer small businesses setting up. There will be a tightening of many sorts on absolutely nonessential items people spend money on.

Knowing this is what is happening in the US - and that it will have some impact on China - we need to take time out to think about what this means for you and our business. What steps do we take now to prepare ourselves for the rippling effect of this? What can we do to make us even more valuable to our clients? More essential? How to position ourselves strategically during this time so that our business thrives in such a climate?

A few thoughts/questions that have gone through my mind:

- *I am delighted to be in China; and in public relations. We are in a growth market in a growth industry and I wouldn't want to be anywhere else at this moment in time.*

- *What are the growth industries we should be focusing on? Things that come to my mind include: Alternative energy (we have strong positioning here in our IR team in Beijing); Technology (should continue to thrive); Healthcare (absolutely essential); Public Affairs (MNCs' thirst for succeeding in China in the wake of the Anti-Monopoly Law); Chinese companies' global expansion opportunities.*

- *Where do we add the most value to our clients? What do they buy and how can we help them even more now when they need us most? Rest assured there will be clients out there that see this time as a huge opportunity and we should be thinking about how companies can take market share in this climate. And you can be comforted in knowing that clients will look for lower cost and more creative marketing possibilities, and we have a huge opportunity to grow with such a dynamic.*

- *What type of "non-essential" items should we look into? Until we see how this will play its way out, we should be cautious with our spending.*

- *And most importantly, where should we be bold? Like skillful Formula One drivers that accelerate around dangerous corners, where do we put on the gas here?*

As all of this unfolds I am a bit edgy. Edgy with worry that this is affecting everyone in many different ways and it will continue to bear its head; and edgy because I can sense opportunity. I was on a call last week with a financial firm. They spoke of concerns, but more of opportunity. They also cautioned to not be frustrated... to look for the opportunities. And that's what I think we need to do.

****

Monday Morning Mail

Year of the Ox a raging bull or sleeping cow? February 3, 2009

Dear Colleagues,

Welcome Back! The Year of the Ox has begun. Is this going to be a "raging bull" year? Or, a sleeping cow year? It's up to us to decide. We had a few wins before the holidays. We have a number of opportunities knocking at our doors and we have the team and brains to make 2009 another record year. This is a bold statement given the tough economic conditions we face, but it is a goal I believe is very much attainable. Today I attended lunch with the Hong Kong office and if you were here with us you would feel the huge confidence and optimism from our Hong Kong colleagues.

With the right tools, collaboration, ambition and hunger, I am sure the year of the Ox for us will be one that we are very proud of. But the work starts now.

****

The global network is a key differentiator, March 23, 2009

Dear Colleagues,

The theme of this week's mail is about the Ogilvy PR Network. I had the wonderful opportunity last week to spend two days in Korea with Chris Graves, our Regional CEO, and Steve Dahloff, our Global head of Strategy and Planning. We were in Korea to meet with a client of Ogilvy PR from the United States. Not only was it good meeting with our global colleagues in Asia, but watching them in action was a huge treat as they prepared their presentation. The chemistry of the team, and the collaboration of everyone would make you proud to be part of this company. The global nature of Ogilvy PR was a major attraction when I joined this company in New York 21 years ago. And for me, this week truly delivered on this. I subsequently had a drink with our Asia Pacific Regional Group CEO, Paul Heath, who with great enthusiasm went on and on about the resources and experience we have in the Ogilvy arsenal in this region and globally. And he asked me, "why don't people tap that more often? This company is all about doing great work for clients. Great work comes from knowledge and insight, yet we often get caught up in our silos without leveraging the strength of the network. We're no better than some independent company if we don't utilize the collective knowledge of this company." As someone who is guilty of often working in my own silo, I couldn't agree more with Paul. If we don't ask, we won't know. It doesn't take a lot of time and we even have tools to help us do so (i.e., New Biz Alerts, Blood Bank, Truffles, O-Village). For, whatever your personal and career goals are at this company, I want to encourage us all to reach out more regularly. If you have a question, ask. Please utilize our global network for your current clients, in new business and to improve your own abilities. This network is one of the treats that comes with employment at Ogilvy PR and it is there for you to leverage.

Environmental Tip of the Week

This coming Saturday (March 28), China will be joining the world in celebrating Earth Hour, a global WWF climate change initiative supported by Ogilvy PR offices around the world. Individuals, businesses, governments and communities are invited to turn out their lights for one hour on Saturday at 8:30 PM to show their support for action on climate change. The event began in Sydney in 2007, when 2 million people switched off their lights. In 2008, more than 50 million people around the globe participated. In 2009, Earth Hour aims to reach out to 1 billion people in 1,000 cities.

****

Forecasting in a volatile environment, May 25, 2009

Dear Colleagues,

The big discussion among the business community these days is what shape the economy in 2009/2010 will form. Is it a L, W, U or V shape? What should we make of this current bounce back and how will this look for the rest of the year? Amidst all of this, we are being asked to do our best to forecast the rest of the year. How do you feel? Are your clients going to do more, less or equal? The first quarter of this year felt very soft. Our clients were holding back to see how Q1 looked. We are seeing more activity now and I certainly hope this will continue.

In the past two weeks we were also brought into a number of crisis discussions in Beijing and Shanghai. And we have been tapped by a few Chinese companies looking to go global. I continue to be cautiously optimistic and I believe we must "stay the course".

I am also perpetually concerned that we are not where we need to be in executing digital programs in Chinese and that is a real priority. We need to quickly build our Ogilvy Earth capability and learn the new tools we have in the Big Ideal and Combustion. That's the future. I also think we need to build into our service a stronger - "outside world" – advisory capability that is not linked to issues and crises. What I mean is something that says to our US clients ... "this week the new US Ambassador was appointed. He speaks Chinese and has an adopted Chinese daughter. He is seen as a good politician in the US and it will be interesting to see how the US-China dynamic will develop. Many countries are angry over a discussed G2 between the US and China. We will watch this and offer thoughts on how this affects your business."

****

Big Picture

Taping interviews and adapting to a more 'self-reliant' China, September 21, 2009

Dear Friends,

I beg each and every one of us to use tape recorders in every interview, discussion or press conference our clients take part in. I witnessed Martin Sorrell in an interview last week with a journalist. Belinda Rabano was taping this. A story came out and it had glaring errors in it. Martin was angry and it became our word vs. the journalist's. The journalist insisted Martin said a certain word, and he was quoted as saying such. Martin said he did not. The interviews were transcribed and we found that Martin did not say the word. If we did not have the tape of this interview, we would have been in much worse shape. It is commonplace now to tape such things and not doing so I feel is unprofessional.

Throughout the last two weeks, there has been a lot of discussion of China's move towards "self-reliance", particularly in advance of the October Holiday. This is playing out in many ways and Joe, Walker and I are putting a paper together for you to share with your clients. Please look for this soon. As public relations counselors, we must root our client communications in the context of the brand world, and having a deep understanding of what is happening and how it impacts our clients is critical to how we deliver what we do.

There is also a heightened degree of conversation around how local multinational companies should be, or what is the right way for an international company to be perceived in China. This is particularly relevant as China moves to more self-reliance. Many experts say that the more a company is part of the fabric of China, providing solutions to address the long-term challenges the country faces, the more these companies will be part of the future of China. Have you thought about how local or international your clients are in this market? How to help them improve? Any suggestions? This is a very rich and hotly debated area and I believe we all need to have our points of view on what route our clients should take.

****

Monday Morning Mail

The importance of being able to write good case studies, October 12, 2009

Dear Friends,

We're going to beat this recession and show the world that the PR business, industry and Ogilvy PR in China can prevail. There is a ton of new business going on, and our existing clients are ramping up activity, so let's show our existing clients why they selected us in the first place. We need to be at our best to close out this year and get us prepared for next year.

I spent the holiday reading more than 500 public relations case studies. I am a judge at this year's Asia PR awards and surprisingly enjoyed this. After closely reading all of the cases I can tell you that 1.) if your campaign does not have an idea around it, it will not have impact; 2.) if you cannot show demonstrable results against campaign objectives a case will not win; and 3) if you can't write a compelling case study that tells a story, you will bore people to death with your work. So please consider these things as you advance in your career. I have always felt that we should use the case study format as a recipe for developing our new business plans, so please also consider this.

****

If you think you're beaten, you are, January 4, 2010

Dear Colleagues,

Welcome to the next decade of the 21st century. What does this decade have in store for you? More importantly, who will determine this?

The first thing I hope each of you do is to reach for the booklet "*The Big IdeaL*" that was given to you. If you don't have this, I will ensure you get a copy. This is both inspiring for us as an organization and for you as a professional. Particularly for us in the public relations industry, we should be masters of the cultural tension section that makes *The Big IdeaL* so powerful. We are entering an age where the marketing and communications disciplines will overlap and we have a lot going in our favor. We need to approach this decade with a fresh perspective, with energy and excitement about what we can do to help our clients' brands succeed.

One thing that struck a cord for me when reading *The Big IdeaL* was the concept of trust. Trust is at the center of any strong brand, company or relationship. This past year, 2009, put great stress on all aspects of trust. We need to get back to a period of unobstructed trust, for ourselves, our relationships with each other, and for our clients. And, this is what I am hoping for us as we approach this new decade.

We have a strong foundation and we have had a period of success. Where to next? I am both anxious and optimistic, appreciative and hungry. I hope you feel similarly.

I spent the holidays with my family, as I hope many of you did. Spending time with my mom, who is a very competitive woman, reminded me of this poem she used to make me read each time I was to compete in sports. This may feel a bit corny, but I thought I would share this as we enter the New Year. Author is unknown.

If You Think You're Beaten

If you think you're beaten, you are,
If you think you dare not, you don't.
If you'd like to win, but think you can't,
It's almost for sure, you won't.

If you think you're losing, you've lost.
For out in the world we find -
Success begins with a person's will,
It's all in the state of mind.

If you think you're outclassed, you are,
You've got to think high to rise.
You have to stay with it,
In order to win the prize.

Life's battles don't always go,
To the one with the better plan.
For more often than not, you will win,
If only you think you can.

****

We must win the digital war battle by battle, May 9, 2011

Dear Friends,

"If you want peace, prepare for war!"

The quote originally expressed in Latin by Publius Flavius Vegetius Renatus began Paul Heath's presentation this last week at the Ogilvy Group's Regional Exco meeting. Paul Heath, for those of you who don't know, is the Regional Ogilvy Group CEO.

The quote was shared as a lead in to a two-day meeting focused on everything digital. I found the two days most informative and alarming, and am further convinced that mastering the world of digital for our clients' communication with their key audience groups is paramount.

We also had a talk by a Business Strategist from Singtel, a Singapore Telcoms operator, who talked about Singtel's transformation. This talk was particularly meaningful to me because I believe we all at Ogilvy PR in China are due for some sort of transformation. I have come to this realization with the help of our own China Exco, given the pressures we are feeling on the business today. Our competition is getting better. Our clients are getting more demanding. Our people (we are the products!) are feeling more and more exhausted. What to do?

I think the challenge is not just Ogilvy PR's challenge, but that of the PR industry. At least the PR industry in North Asia. We need to ensure PR is at the Boardroom table. That we are a critical part of any marketing campaign, and not an add-on. If we are demanding fees that reflect a "Best of Class" consultancy, we need to deliver against these. We somehow need to move up the value chain and to move up quickly.

As we begin to think about this there are a few things that are central to the next phase of PR in North Asia, or Ogilvy PR in North Asia.

- *The first thing is digital and all things digital. Digital competence, success, strategy and execution will be vital. We must win the digital war, battle by battle!*
- *Brand strategy and differentiation will also be critical and how brands build value for our clients in the digital world.*
- *A deep understanding of the "cultural tension" in each of our markets will be important, as this is part of The Big IdeaL and is the part PR professionals should be best at. Our thinking process about the "Brand World" fits in well here and must be leveraged to give us competitive advantage.*

- *Certainly great writing (content generation based on a client's message structure) and storytelling skills will be the underpinning of whatever we are trying to create or sell. I cannot underscore enough the importance of improving our own fundamentals as we enter new territories.*
- *Finally, your own relationship network will be important, and translates into how quickly you can call up people of influence and involve them in your clients' campaigns.*

What is exciting is that Ogilvy's own *Big IdeaL* will not change and is completely relevant for the future. That is "Ogilvy believes the world will be a better place if we could bring out the inner greatness in brands, companies and people."

Our challenge is working towards *The Big IdeaL*, using the tools, information, trainings, and people inside and outside this company to do this. It is not going to be easy by any means. And my task, and that of the regional Exco leaders - your PR Exco leaders - will be working towards this. I hope you are all charged up about this as I am.

I won't share anything more this week. I think the above is enough for us to ponder. In the words of Peter Drucker, the well-known management guru, "The best way to predict the future is to create it."

****

What we decide to do and not to do are equally important, July 18, 2011

Dear Friends,

Reflection. Are we finding enough time to step back and reflect on what we are doing, how we are doing it, whether it is adding value, and to consider other creative and effective ways to drive results for our clients?

I feel that the next stage of development in the PR industry is an "open field" and I would like us to define it. We have some spots of real leadership... work we are doing in the digital space, our nation's branding work for Chengdu, our creative marketing and corporate positioning work... but this is only a start. I am also delighted that we were the first to set up a China Practice in the US (which other firms are beginning to follow), and to also be the first International PR firm to establish in Mongolia. These are small moves in the grand scheme of things, but they are keeping us ahead of the curve on where opportunities are presenting themselves.

Back to "reflection." I hope everyone will take time away to think about your life, work, the impact you are having, what you want for yourselves, and more. Working flat out for a year is not healthy and you must get away to find and explore new ideas.

As we cross the mid-year point I also want us to instill a "challenger" mindset into the North Asia operations. In my view, challengers are hungry, and they are willing to dig, dig, dig to find insights. They have focus and a will to win and succeed. I say that because when we are focused, and want to win, we have the team, resources and organization to do so. And when we are not interested, or half-interested, or when we are facing client difficulties, we struggle to succeed. I believe in North Asia, "what we decide TO do, and what we decide NOT to do are equally important." This past month in China we have told a few long-term clients we are not interested in working with them any more. In explaining why to one of the clients, the senior manager asked, "why didn't you bring this to me earlier?" The reasons behind this are long and detailed and I won't belabor this, but it sends a signal that I think is important. We must be cautious in how we do this, because I do not want us to be viewed as arrogant or disinterested. And, we will not grow and succeed by turning away business. Rather, I would like to explore all angles and then decide if a particular client is right for us. We do not need to do everything, but we should also have a clear mind about who we want to work with, what we have to offer and why it will be valuable to them in the short and long term.

The final thing I would like us to contemplate and to ask ourselves is this: "Do you have real, true, deep knowledge of the media in our markets?" In China, this is a frequent "doubt" our clients share with us. Since many of our clients regularly come to us for "positioning" and "media knowledge and insight" we must be sure we are really the most knowledgeable and insightful in the market. If not, please consider what we should do to get there. We have a few new hires that bring particular expertise in this area and it is proving to be extremely valuable. I am thinking about how to institutionalize this, but we need fast action here.

****

Big Picture

Clients, people, work – if we get these three things right, we're golden,
January 14, 2013

A belated very Happy New Year to you! While you and I may not be able to determine everything that is in store for us, we certainly can affect the route we take and what the possible results will be. I love this time of the year because we have a clean slate in front of us and all of the opportunity as long as we are willing, able and motivated to go after what we want for ourselves. So I hope this month you are thinking through your personal and professional goals and making plans to attack these. Please do not expect anyone to do this for you and do not blame anyone for the lack of progress against these. No one will look after you like you must, and I hope you are ready and energized to make 2013 an important and exciting year. Please don't wait until tomorrow to do what you can do today.

On Friday I had the opportunity to join Miles Young, Chris Graves, Joe Zhou and Lyndon Cao in a meeting and dinner in New York with a senior government delegation from Sichuan Province. Our client from Chengdu joined this meeting and she was most complimentary about the work Ogilvy PR has done in branding Chengdu. Thank you team Chengdu. The delegation outlined a number of opportunities for us, particularly around the FORTUNE Global Forum that will take place in June of this year. Miles communicated that the Ogilvy Group will have its board meeting in Chendgu in May and that we are gearing up for a fantastic year. The Chengdu work has been world class and we just need more of this coming from each of our offices, practices and teams.

We enter 2013 with a strong foundation and also ambitious new business targets. The principles of our business are quite simple. We need to have great clients that are interested in partnership and working together to create world-class work. We need outstanding, proactive, creative, positive and hard working staff to deliver this work. And we need to develop the creative campaigns that delight our clients and attract new clients, that instill pride in our staff, and that pay handsomely so we can share that fortune with our people and our investors. Clients. People. Work. If we get the combination of these three things right, we're golden. These principles apply to everyone. We are all part of this equation so as we tackle 2013, please think about clients, people, work and please be prepared to do your share. Please also do not forget that beyond the work are people that allow us to do what we do. So take time for your families as well as I believe a very happy family will help you in all aspects of life.

****

Monday Morning Mail

The future belongs to agile businesses and people who just get stuck in, July 15, 2013

One of my most favorite quotes is from the management guru, Peter Drucker, who once said, "the best way to predict the future is to create it."

Well there is nothing more energizing for me than spending a few days discussing your, our and my future with some of the best and brightest people in the public relations business. And that is what Debby and I did this past week in Los Angeles. Chris Graves, our Global CEO, brought together around 30 people from our global operations to discuss the future. Steve Dahllof was there. So was Thomas Crampton and Marion McDonald from Asia, and Kieran Moore, group head of Ogilvy PR from Australia. We were a contingent of seven from Asia. Based on the work, growth, prospects, structures of our business and more, it is clear that in the world of public relations "the world is definitely flat."

Some of the conclusions from the meeting pointed to the fact that the future will be determined not by one geography or another, but by businesses that are agile, hungry, creative and by people who just get stuck in! That means people who get things done. Data-driven decisionmaking, an area we have a lot to learn about, will be central. So will content. We heard about a content factory in our London office that Debby and I are considering replicating for China. We talked about incubating creative units to tease out new areas of expertise. We discussed the network and its importance and how to make all of us net more. And we listened to a talk by Ben Richards, who shared where Fusion has grown to and how it has helped win bigger and more valuable engagements. There is a lot to share that we will do in the months to come and you will see progress from this gathering help to guide our future strategy. We are also coming back with some valuable IP Chris Graves has developed around behavioral science that is most applicable to our business. One thing this meeting also did for me was underscore the importance of getting people together and we must work to make sure we connect at every chance we get. Strong networks are built by people and the connections they make and these take work. So please be most generous with your time, sharing your thoughts etc. to continue to make this network net.

****

The power of emotion and how we package what we do, September 23, 2013

On the eve of the Mid-Autumn Festival, a group of us gathered in Shanghai to attend the Asia Pacific Sabre Awards, one of the major award competitions celebrating the best in public relations. As I sat there, I had a moment of reflection on where we are in our business and where we are going. This reflection was not about revenue or clients. It was about the fundamental shift I feel is taking place. I had just finished a week of presentations and client workshops and there was one thing that kept poking at me... and that was the "power of emotion!"

As PR professionals we have grown used to thinking in multiple messages... factual evidence that supports a certain brand claim our clients are making. And while facts and evidence form the foundation of what makes a strong brand, without "emotion" the strength of the brand will always come in question. So for some of us who like facts without the drama, we need to work on the art and skill of packaging facts to evoke emotion. For me, this is what The Big IdeaL is all about and the better we are at developing these, the quicker we will climb the value chains of our clients. The intersect for us with other disciplines in the future is how we hone the skill of messaging to bring about powerful emotion to help our clients tell engaging stories that build their brands. Think: Evidence. Emotion. Big IdeaL. Storytelling. This is a very rich area and I believe we are only at the beginning of understanding the connections between these things that combine to influence behavior.

The other epiphany I had this week was around the topic of packaging. I worry a lot about how we package our ideas and communicate them to achieve the proper emotional response. Great packaging aids our overall ability to tell stories and I fear we are very weak in how we package what we do. You will hear a lot more about this in the days to come.

So think "emotion", think "packaging" and please take time to think about how we address and improve both areas in the future.

****

Monday Morning Mail

Stepping up to a broader, regional role, December 30, 2013

The end of this year marks a full 18 years for me in China. Beginning Wednesday I will take on the broader Asia Pacific leadership role for Ogilvy PR, but I cannot do so without saying a huge THANK YOU to everyone in North Asia. Success in this business is not the result of one person. Certainly there are standout stars in all of our businesses, but it is my belief that it is the collective "whole" that makes us truly remarkable. We have had a year of award wins and recognition in all of our offices. We've won a lot of new business, attracted some very capable new staff, advanced our social capabilities and executed well for our clients across the board. I often reflect on what we have created and marvel at how lucky and fortunate we are. So thank you everyone for what you have done.

Going into my 19th year and my 27th with Ogilvy PR, I am feeling very energetic. We are on the cusp of a major shift in our business. There is a mash-up of marketing disciplines that is resulting in clients saying they want a solution and they don't care where this is going to come from. Paul Heath, our Group CEO for Asia Pacific, speaks often about the dissolution of disciplines and the evolution of multifaceted solutions that solve our clients' problems. I believe we are strongly placed to excel in that new dynamic. It takes new skills (analytics for example) and some refined old skills (content generation) to make us fly. We also need to find a way to talk about this so that we can win a disproportionate share of the opportunities. I cannot think of a better industry to be in at a more opportune time in our development located in a more robust part of the world. The stars are aligning!

All is not perfect, however. If we let the challenges presented by our size and matrix get in the way of what we need to do for our clients, this would be a real shame. If we don't listen to what clients need and lead them, we will soon be obsolete. If we don't recognize that everyone wants what we have, we will be foolish. To be a leader in our industry we need to recognize that there are expectations of us that are shaped by every conversation, communication and campaign. There are going to be people all around us trying to bring us down. We need to be aware of this, but we need single-minded focus that we exist to bring out the inner greatness in brands, companies, institutions and people. Great PR firms and PR professionals are influential and we must operate at the very core of influence.

What excites me is the opportunity to use our skills to help clients win in this new dynamic. There is no better place to do this with so many capable people as we have at Ogilvy. So thank you for everything you have done. I will expand the *Monday Morning Mail* to all of our Asia Pacific brothers and sisters, but for all of you who make up the North Asia community, I just want to say thank you for everything you do, have done and will do for us in the future. Once again, in the words of Peter Drucker, "The best way to predict the future is to create it."

Big Picture

Insightful and effective campaigns that are talked about, February 3, 2014

Cultural Influence! The focus of this week's *Monday Morning Mail* is about our work product and the importance of creating campaigns so insightful and effective that they penetrate the societies in which we live. Ogilvy PR's global work for the National Heart, Lung and Blood Institute known as the "Heart Truth Campaign" and symbolized by the "Red Dress" is one example of this. This campaign changed the way women view heart disease in the United States and beyond. Also, I would argue the Chengdu Pambassadors campaign was talked about well beyond what we imagined. Our colleagues in Europe announced the first lab-grown beef patty for Maastricht University that had cultural influence. This event made news around the world last year as the university carved out a reputation for solving the world's future food security needs. I saw the news everywhere before finding out that it was done by our colleagues in Europe.

I am reminded of this because I am in Taiwan right now and a Taiwan advertising campaign launched for Ta Chong Bank was the prime example of cultural influence. I was literally walking down a bike path and heard an older gentleman talking about this campaign. It is a beautifully done film and features a number of octogenarians putting their lives on hold to relive days of the past. The campaign was centered around the idea that Ta Chong was a bank for ordinary people with extraordinary dreams.

Ogilvy is known for such campaigns that are "talked about." IBM's Smarter Planet is one of those. So is the "Campaign for Real Beauty" we created for Dove.

Can your campaign be next? What we need is a great insight mixed with a good idea perfectly executed. I hope you will keep this top of mind as we develop our client campaigns in the coming year.

****

Monday Morning Mail

Competition for leadership in the new era, April 14, 2014

We began the year with a few goals. Growth was one of them. A quest for market-influencing work that will make us famous, be fun to work on and pay us well (fortune) was another. I am happy to report that as we go market-by-market these goals are proving possible. In China we have won a number of IPOs of Chinese companies who will be listing on the US exchanges shortly. We have broadened our healthcare business in China, and we successfully handled a potentially volatile crisis in a second-tier Chinese city together with our colleagues in Japan.

The competition for leadership in the new era of marketing and communications is happening NOW. If we don't hone our brand consulting and social offerings now... it is going to be too late. I have had a number of conversations with clients about helping them manage and lead their brands across multiple traditional and new media channels and there is demand here. The firm that wins will be the one which brings it all together and has great, simple examples that demonstrate how it can be done. And that must be us. We have some expertise in the network that is helping with this and I am anxious that we accelerate our competencies and abilities to deliver these services. That is what is keeping me up at night right now. How fast can we as a network lead the industry in this new marketing era?

****

Crafting rational and emotional messages that cut through the clutter, November 17, 2014

So I am sitting at my desk on Friday morning and Andrew Dunn, a very smart colleague of ours who leads one of our tech clients in China, comes over and says, "I think we live in a world void of facts anymore. It seems anyone can take any information and do whatever they want with it and all truth and reality ceases to exist."

His comment comes at the end of a week where the US President, Barack Obama, headlined his speech at the APEC summit reciting former Chinese leader Deng Xiaoping's famous quote, "We must find truth from the facts."

And the week before I had the privilege of being in the company of our Global Chairman, Chris Graves, on his tour of Asia. Chris spoke at the Ford PR Leaders Conference and shared his thinking on human behavior and decision-making and the role of the right/left brain rational and emotional influence on decisions.

Facts. Truth. Rational. Emotional. Decision-Making. Behavior. It was a heavy two weeks; a period that was also shaped by the visits to China of almost all of the Asia Pacific leaders. I had the honor of listening live to speeches of Obama and Putin, and witnessed the introduction to the world stage of Joko Widodo, the new President of Indonesia. What is clear to me, more than anything else, is the importance of the message and the delivery in such globally important meetings, and the role that open dialogue and communication plays. I left the APEC meeting feeling more optimistic than ever before about the communications industry and the important role we have. How we help our clients craft messages that are both rational and emotional, that cut through the clutter and are based on facts and truth is the new normal.

****

Curiosity is a common characteristic among the best professionals in the public relations business.

Chapter Seven

Learning

Pursue knowledge the way a pig pursues truffles, June 30, 2008

Dear Friends,

On October 11, 1978 David Ogilvy wrote a memo to the Board of Ogilvy & Mather.

A Teaching Hospital

I have a new metaphor.

Great Hospitals do two things: They look after patients, and they teach young doctors.

Ogilvy & Mather does two things: We look after clients, and we teach young advertising people.

Ogilvy & Mather is the teaching hospital of the advertising world. And, as such; to be respected above all other agencies.

One of the underlying characteristics that define the great Ogilvy people I have known is curiosity. They thirst for new knowledge and new ways of doing things and in the words of David Ogilvy, "We pursue knowledge the way a pig pursues truffles."

So it is in this spirit that I write to you all because I am worried. I worry that we are just too busy to step back, learn new things and to attend the company training programs designed specifically for all of you. We had a number of trainings taking place last week whereby the Ogilvy PR people put forward for these did not show up. There were some cases where we didn't even let the trainer know. Now these programs cost us money, and what is more, they have been created with great care and thought for what we all need to do to build our skills. I know you are all busy and I appreciate the care and concern you are giving your clients, but not attending is a missed opportunity at best, and not letting the instructors know is simply disrespectful.

You should know that last year when we put the budgets together for this and we needed to make some cuts in investment, Miles, TB and Shenan insisted that we preserve the training budget. The vision is that this is what sets us apart from others. So, we have not invested in some things, and we are spending money on training that seems to not be valued.

So here's what we are going to do: we are going to make attendance at such trainings conditional on the participant's agreement that you are going to show up and attend throughout (barring any absolute emergency). Selection of who goes and who does not will be given much more careful consideration.

I fear what will happen is that soon we will have clients who need solutions and if we do not continually learn, we'll be history. We all must make this a priority and I am looking to all of you to help in this regard.

****

Beijing Olympics a fine example of worldwide messaging, August 11, 2008

Dear Friends,

Today, a quick note from your sleep deprived author.

The Past Week

Friday evening at 8:08:08 marked the much awaited opening ceremonies and it was everything it was built up to be. People from all over the world remarked how wonderful it was and my wife and I had the honor to be in attendance to watch it. For those that missed this, I am sure there will be a DVD sold and if you want to understand how an event can serve to send a message to the world, well buy some popcorn, sit in front of the TV and watch this. I was very excited to be there and proud to have lived in Beijing for the past eight years in anticipation of this.

With the Opening behind us and the Games underway, I would like everyone who is in Beijing to take time to observe your surroundings. With 70,000 volunteers it seems everyone is anxious to practice their English, security guards are working to make your life easy and the subway works remarkably well. It is all much more than I had expected and I hope you all get to witness this.

Learning

> Environmental Tip of the Week
>
> Could we all try to take some form of mass transportation this week? I have been relying on this for all of my Olympics transportation needs and it has been a wonderful experience.

****

Let's redefine "Shanzhai", December 15, 2008

Dear Colleagues:

Where do you get your ideas? I think this is something each of us should reflect upon as we enter the new year. Some of you may get these from books, others from TV, movies or the Internet, and others through friends. I would say that I get most of mine through "conversations." This last week was filled with conversations with a number of different people, from many different angles. I spoke with an optimistic young recruit about his pursuit of a job. I studied our sports business with the Director of Ogilvy Sports as my teacher. I listened to a speech by a well-known economist about the impact of this financial crisis. Lunched with the Ogilvy Group's Anthony Wong, our Digital Acceleration Director, about the work he does. Met with Canon in a 360 opportunity. And the list goes on. The point here is that through these conversations and more I get my ideas. And because I learn so much through these conversations, I feed off of them in my day-to-day work. I encourage you, and beg you, to get out from behind your desks, to circulate in the office and in your cities and have conversations with different people. We are advisors who are expected to understand the world around our clients' business and in my opinion this understanding comes from circulating and conversations.

So what themes jump out from this past week's conversations:

- *Value - In the wake of all of the bad news about the global economy, what clients want to talk about is value. What "real" value are you bringing your clients and how effective is this. Today more than ever before what people want is value and if we cannot articulate this before we speak to our clients, we are in trouble.*

Monday Morning Mail

- *Storytelling - How to get your point across by making it interesting. I sat through two presentations this week. One by a banker to a bunch of CFOs. People left and no one listened. The other was us, doing a 360 credential presentation. Have you ever sat through a comprehensive 360 presentation? You can learn a lot... and get confused. Every Ogilvy company has its own tools and philosophies, subsidiary companies and differentiators, and by the end of the presentation I was confused. It made me think even harder about how we talk about what we do, make it interesting and make it easy to comprehend.*

This Week in Resource Sharing

The latest issue of Cool Path by Discovery Team is now available. This year, our life is full of Shanzhai (fake and knockoff commodities and cultural products) elements: Shanzhai cellular phones, Shanzhai stars, Shanzhai TV programs. Today, "Shanzhai" has become such a popular term in China. In this issue, let's redefine "Shanzhai" and dig out what it has brought for us. Please take a look at these wonderful insights brought to us by the Discovery Unit.

Environmental Tip of the Week

With this week's *Monday Morning Mail* I am asking Toni to coordinate with all of the office managers in each of our offices to consider doing away with the use of paper plates and plastic utensils for monthly meetings and celebrations, and to purchase enough dining ware for the offices so that we can re-use these.

****

Learning

Learning from a geophysicist about tsunami and earthquake prediction, February 9, 2009

Dear Friends,

Sometimes pleasures in life come in small doses at the most unexpected times. I am sitting on a plane to the US right now next to a Dr. Walter Mooney, a Geophyscist and the Lead Coordinator for the US Government for the Indian Ocean Tsunami Warning System. This guy is one of the most senior scientists in the US Government responsible for forecasting earthquakes and tsunamis and helping to train people throughout the world on how to understand such natural disasters and how to prevent tragedies in such a case. Now, I normally don't spend a huge amount of time bothering my neighbor on the long-haul flights, but we spoke for nearly an hour and he fascinated me with his experiences. He has spent a lot of time in Sichuan and has many, many friends in China. He told me the Chinese government is really very serious about making sure Sichuan never happens again. He told me that in the next decade we may see an earthquake in the Hayward Fault of San Francisco, an earthquake near Burma, and possibly a tsunami in the Pacific near Alaska that will head south to Hawaii. He showed me a video of the work they are doing in the Indian ocean to help Southeast Asia prepare for such issues.

This guy is full of energy and passion and you would have enjoyed hearing his stories about the work he is doing in Indonesia, India, Afghanistan and China. He suggested I check out a YouTube video he made himself in Sichuan called "Beichuan Earthquake". Janet, remind me to tell you about the conversation we had about his views on Taipei 101 and the Mori Building. Chris Graves once asked who was the most fascinating person that you have ever sat next to on a plane and this guy probably ranks up there.

So in the spirit of the environment, passion and predicting the future, one highlight from this week was the amount of email going through the Ogilvy system on the development of a Sustainability Practice. I am sharing in this note some of the materials that have been making their way through the system.

Personally, I had the opportunity to spend time in the Hong Kong office and with the iPR leadership. What a delight! Clara was kind enough to invite me to the post-CNY (Chinese New Year) luncheon and I could feel the passion from this office during the luncheon. There is great confidence in this office with a strong client list. Among the larger clients are Disneyland, Nokia and adidas. And we should be thankful to these folks (Azwar!) for farming and taking care of such regional clients as Novell and UPS.

Monday Morning Mail

> ### Environmental Tip of the Week
>
> Buy yourself a re-usable cup this week and bring this to Starbucks instead of using their take-out paper cups. With as much coffee as some of you drink you can save a tree by eliminating this waste.

****

Contributing to the health and welfare of clients' brands, April 13, 2009

Dear Friends,

This past week the famous Intel Developer Forum took place and the love coming from Intel to Ogilvy would make everyone proud. Thank you Intel Team. Google launched its music channel with huge success, and I know there is a ton of other things taking place in all of our offices that are contributing to the health and welfare of our clients' brands. That's what we do, right?

My one personal lesson over the last two weeks came in a presentation to a very sophisticated western client who asked some pretty challenging questions to TB, Mickey Chak and me. The questions: "What does humor mean to the Chinese? What is the role of religion? What is going to happen 20 years out when the full spectrum of the one-child policy is felt?" It made me think that we must do a much better job of explaining China to the outside world beyond the obvious. The economic numbers don't tell a story like a deep description of a modern Chinese family and what they think, feel and believe. Our insights and thinking must go much deeper and our points of view must be much more robust. So with that, I encourage you to think about the world you live in and ask the question of why? Why, why, why? Only by being curious will our explanations be much more thorough.

****

Learning

What separates people who 'really know their stuff' from the bullshitters, April 27, 2009

Dear Friends,

I am frustrated and I hope you are too! Frustrated that there is so much great information in this company and I have so little time and capacity to absorb it all. Actually, this is the beauty of this company isn't it? There is just so much juicy, good stuff coming through the system. And if you reach out just a little bit, someone has information somewhere in this company. I certainly hope that when your clients call you for hard-to-find information, that somewhere in this company you can find the answer. I know that I am rarely disappointed if I really search for things at Ogilvy.

So, why this topic this week? Because on Tuesday, April 21 in Beijing I organized an Integration Day. A day whereby nine companies that are part of, or affiliated with, Ogilvy came together to present what they do and how they do it. It was a fascinating experience and it was fun observing how our sister companies present themselves. I also learned a ton. I learned how absolutely important the presentation and articulation of cases are. I feel we do these all wrong, by the way. I learned how beautifully some people present things and how others are sloppily thrown together. I learned who the people are that really know their stuff, and who are the bullshitters. And, I came to the conclusion that winning new business and your client's confidence involves a combination of good ideas, packaging and a confident presenter. I certainly hope we all consider these things and work to be the best communications agency in China.

****

Remaining connected, July 6, 2009

Today you are receiving a very abbreviated *Monday Morning Mail*. I miss you all, and I remain connected,... One thing I do know is that sometimes you need to get away to see the world in a different way and I have new ideas coming to me everyday.

****

Being the child who knows no fear, June 4, 2012

Are we too old to learn? I think we all need to think about this. I am just back from Kyoto Japan where for four days I participated in an Ogilvy senior management conference to learn the latest and greatest of what is happening in the world of marketing and communications. I love these conferences because they serve as a sort of "renewal" for me. I arrive early and take a good seat and make sure I don't miss out on anything that is being presented. TB once suggested to me that in these conferences we should "suspend judgment". We should stop thinking "this is good" or "this is bad". But, rather "this is interesting, what can we learn from this." And that is what this conference has done for me. And now it is available to all of you on the Ogilvy website. Paul Heath, our Asia Pacific CEO, also sent you emails everyday to explain what was happening. He knows that the company isn't run by those people in Kyoto alone and he stressed how important it was that all of you get access to these presentations as well. I particularly enjoyed Rory Sutherland's talk on behavioral economics and Anthony Wong and Tim Broadbent's presentation on Creativity and Effectiveness.

One thing that made me very proud was that among some 15 Young Stars that were selected to attend this conference, Joyce Qiu from Ogilvy PR in Shanghai and Olivia Fang, from Ogilvy PR in Beijing won the right to attend by participating in the creativity contest. They had to submit a video about what creativity means to them. Please join me in congratulating them and thanking them for their strong representation of us.

On the third day these Young Stars were able to present to the group and Olivia shared this passage with all of us:

> *I have never felt this anxious.*
> *I am anxious because I am no longer the child who knows no fear.*
>
> *I feel old when my dreams are too realistic.*
> *I feel old when I fear to be the crazy one.*
> *I feel old when experience, rather than my heart, is guiding my journey.*
>
> *Unsuccessful living is nothing different from dying.*
>
> *Let's try to live again, truthfully,*
> *by being the child who knows no fear.*

****

Learning

Continuous learning is something we all must do, November 6, 2012

The story of Ogilvy PR North Asia in 2012 has pretty much been written, and I am now focused on finishing the year respectably and preparing for 2013. What is your story for 2012? Have you had a good year? What did you accomplish and what do you feel you wish you did more of? I find this time of the year a good time to reflect and to spend the final two months addressing some of the things you wish you had accomplished but have not. The one area I hope all of us consider is to ask the question to ourselves, "what are we doing on our own to learn new things?" There are enough resources at this company to learn something new every day. If you go to Ogilvydo.com there are resources there. Truffles or O-Village are other useful platforms. If you are in China and read Graham's "Little Gifts" there are lessons there. There is something to learn about brands and their online engagement everyday at this company, and this discipline is evolving even as I write this. If you are a foreigner, there are opportunities to learn new things about the language of the country you are living in. I try to pick up a new word in every Chinese meeting I attend. If you are a native speaker in your designated country, make it a point to learn and improve your English language skills as part of the Ogilvy PR network. My point here is that "continuous learning" is something we all must do. It is part of the Ogilvy culture, and it is up to each of us to take responsibility for this. Ogilvy can bring you learning opportunities, but it is up to us to make use of them.

My second message is about recognizing what we have and giving thanks. As I watch the television and witness the devastation in New York and New Jersey, and as I speak to my brother who has been without power for a week, I am reminded at how fortunate we are to have some of the basic necessities of life: food, water, transport, heat. What is remarkable is that until you are stripped of these, it is easy to take them all for granted. But people in the Greater New York area, where all of life's necessities are plentiful, are doing without. If you are having a bad day because your computer is slow to boot up, or you have too much to do, or the line is too long at Starbucks, my suggestion is to just take a step back and consider what is really important. How often do we celebrate consuming a nice glass of water in the morning? There are people in this world that do not have this luxury. Enjoy your luxuries and appreciate them!

Have a great week folks. Please think through what you can do to accelerate your learning and be thankful for what you have, not what you are without.

****

Monday Morning Mail

The importance of 'losing' and learning from losing, April 1, 2013

This *Monday Morning Mail* is dedicated to the important subject of "LOSING." Let me begin by first saying that I hope no one ever categorizes you as a "loser." And while I hope we do have some losses in our basket, may these be very few and minor. Yet, "losing" and learning from losing is a very important discipline. I was reminded of this during a client conference I attended this week with one of our very important clients. They are religious about understanding their competition and learning about how they win and lose. The Chairman of this company spoke about being competitive and worrying to a point of paranoia. Just after he spoke I saw this quote from, I believe it was, Bill Gates on twitter, "Your unhappy customers are your greatest source of learning." And then I thought about us.

None of us in North Asia have a 100% win record, and if we do that is a problem. It is a problem because we may not be pushing the limits enough. While our objective is to win a disproportionate share of the opportunities we compete for, we need to study our loses very closely, understand the competition and learn from these. Sometimes we will lose because of chemistry. Other times, because our ideas are not creative enough or we are not strategic enough. Or, sometimes it is because we are too expensive. We can lose for a variety of factors and the more due diligence we do upfront when we invest in new business, the better off it will be for the client and for ourselves.

I was reminded of this also this past week because I met with a client who will be issuing an RFP next week. I visited their office and had a casual conversation. We did some research in advance, I did my own research on the clients we would meet, and we had a very productive, casual conversation. We are well primed to receive this RFP and while the competition has not begun, I feel we are in a good position with this prospect. Nothing can replace the deep due diligence we must do in advance of any pitch and I personally believe that only when you feel you can't go any deeper will real opportunity evolve.

So the message here is to let's limit our losses, but when we do lose, let's dig in deep to find out as much as possible. And when we do go for opportunity we need to work very hard to put ourselves in a position of strength.

****

Relationships

The greatest joy in the public relations business will be found in the relationships you develop.

Chapter Eight

Relationships

Ending an abusive relationship, June 16, 2008

Friends,

We learned a lot from dealing with one of our largest client's procurement departments this week and I expect we will see more of such type of situations in the future. What we have learned also in such negotiation is the importance of separating emotion in such circumstances. Great PR people have a great understanding of emotion. We need to so we know how to craft messages that cut through. But we also need to be grounded in the rational. Having a proper balance of both is extremely important.

We also resigned a client in the IR team. After months of what I would term an abusive relationship, we told the client that we were going to end our partnership. According to David Ogilvy, "you can't build a business by firing clients", but sometimes I believe we must take a stand. I think all of us should do our utmost to work out our relationships with our clients, and to have honest discussions, but we also sometimes must make difficult decisions. In China, what you do and don't do are equally important, and this is a client that I just think we will be better off without. For those in the IR team who worked on this client, my special thanks to all of you.

Environmental Tip of the Week

The below comes from the New York office. I would like us all to respond if you could please.

As our society becomes more "eco-friendly" and educated on the effects of global warming, millions of people are taking actions to fight it - switching to renewable energy, using Energy Star appliances, carpooling and more. In a few sentences, tell us your story about what you, your family, or friends are doing to fight global warming and your story may become part of a campaign for the Environmental Defense Fund and help one of Ogilvy's pro bono clients! Please reply to Sarah Rinehimer at sarah.rinehimer@ogilvy.com.

Please also take the time to switch off your computer at night. As I walk through the office I see a number of desktops still on. Please do so at the end of the day before leaving your desk for the evening.

Relationships

Beijing Olympics closing, Shanghai World Financial Center opening, September 1, 2008

Dear Colleagues,

What a show! After seven years of preparation and 16 days of excitement the Beijing 2008 Olympic Games have come to a close. For me personally this seven years was a fantastic journey which taught me many things. I believe the true story of the Olympics has yet to be fully told and that is of China's transformation. I can tell you from the comments I received from people watching all over the world, they were impressed and they saw a China that is rarely portrayed in the foreign press. It is incumbent on all of us as communicators to keep these lines of communication open.

The Past Week

We must now move on from the Olympics and it feels like life is getting back to normal in Beijing. Those plans that were put on hold are being activated and we're now in a four-month sprint to the end of the year. On Friday, I sat with the management team and reviewed Q3 and we are doing well to date, but have forecasted a lot of new business in the coming months. Please work closely with your Directors to close the new business gaps. I also had the honor and privilege to go to the opening of the Shanghai World Financial Center on Thursday. This was the largest press conference I have ever seen (some 400+ journalists) and credit goes to Janet and the team. I loved watching Janet try to coordinate the television and photographers for the photoshoot. If you are in Shanghai, you must go to this building and walk round the observatory. This is the largest building in Asia (101 floors). We also had a number of younger staff in Shanghai sent home by the client for the way they were dressed. We must all realize that we are asking to be treated like professionals and charging professional fees and the client expectations are very high. Getting how we dress right is simple and we must learn from this.

Environmental Tip of the Week

Check your car tire pressure regularly. Under-inflation increases tire wear, reduces your fuel economy by up to 3% and leads to higher greenhouse gas emissions and releases of air pollutants.

****

Tell me who your friends are and I will tell you who you are, May 24, 2010

Dear Friends,

The topic of this *Monday Morning Mail* is about "Relationships." I am writing not about "business relationships" that often translate into your network of influence. I am focusing on the quality of your "personal relationships" and asking you to think about these in the context of your life. For many of us, or me at least, our work is very much a center of our lives. Whether we like it or not, we spend a lot of time at the office or in the company of people who are in someway related to Ogilvy. I am often reminded how lucky I am to have met so many great people at Ogilvy. And, the people who have come and gone remain some of my closest friends. What is central about these relationships is that they do not come down to what someone can do for you, they are rather a statement about what type of person you are. And so my message is to remind us of "where we have come from" and the people who have been influential in that journey and to make sure those people are priorities in your life.

Heavy? This is not intended to be. However, this month we re-welcomed to China Marcia Silverman, Ogilvy PR's Chairman, who I would describe as the queen of "quality relationships". For those that missed the staff meeting in Beijing, Marcia is a 29-year employee of Ogilvy PR. She has risen up from the ranks where many of us are today. And in all of my dealings with her over the past 23 years, no conversation has ever started with "how is x client, or y client?" They begin with, "how is your wife and your kids?" She lightens up when she talks about people at Ogilvy with whom she has worked, and when she talks about her own family. And she has a quiet way of letting you know that the real recipe to success is to get your relationship house in order ... and all else will follow. My mother is also in Beijing this month and she has a statement, "tell me who your friends are and I will tell you who you are." Same message. And while we welcomed these visitors, I had a late night drink with a close friend from my days in Taiwan, who is exploring the China market for his new business. Ching Ping and other colleagues offered him an overview of the China luxury market, in which we may help him launch a product. And while I am excited about the new business prospect, I enjoyed reliving our days in Taiwan and knowing somehow something I am doing can help him. So the question I am asking myself that I would suggest each of us asks, is "what have you done for your friends lately that has no ask related to it?" Think about it. Ogilvy's former Chairwoman, Charlotte Beers, once said in a conference that she felt "generosity" was her secret for success and I hope each of us is generous in cultivating and preserving our relationships.

Relationships

The power of random acts of kindness, March 3, 2014

A few stories for this *Monday Morning Mail* to begin our week.

The first is themed, "Generosity!" Years ago when I was young and just starting to work in Asia, I was invited to a regional group meeting when Charlotte Beers was Ogilvy's global CEO. Someone asked her what she felt was the "secret to success" in our business. Without missing a beat she answered, "simple generosity." "Be generous with your people, with your time and with your advice to clients," was her response. Of all the meetings I have attended I remembered that comment particularly. I truly believe if we are generous with each other, with our clients and with our time for our colleagues, families, friends and loved ones, that is the first ingredient for success. Personally, I believe "random acts of kindness" are much more powerful than the things we are expected to do, so please consider. That is:

Message 1 for this week: think about your own generous pursuits and please make them part of your success.

Message 2 is something I learned from Andrew Thomas this week and it is about optimism and belief. On tour with Andrew in Manila and Vietnam, he shared a story which many of you may have heard. The story goes like this: "Two brothers, who are sons of an Italian shoe salesman, are dispatched to an emerging market. They arrive and not one person in the country wears shoes. The first son calls his father and says, 'Dad, I am coming home. There is no market for shoes in this country.' The second calls home and says, 'Dad, send more shoes. As many as you can find. No one has shoes in this market.'" In our business, we make things happen from nothing. Our ideas are our currency, and I hope we become more like the second son in the story above.

Message 3 is something I read from the *New York Times* about questioning our habits and processes. There was a feature on an executive who said that his one critical life story came from riding a bus with his mother one day. He explained for the longest time he took a bus from one stop to another and everyone got on and off at the designated stops. One day he was riding with his mother and she asked the bus driver if he could stop in the middle of two stops so she could go to a supermarket nearby. The bus driver stopped at the unconventional stop and every passenger got off. His lesson: "sometimes you have to question what you are doing to ensure it is the most effective and efficient way."

Thanks for all you do. Be generous. Be optimistic. Question the norm.

****

Monday Morning Mail

Client chemistry, communities and talent, August 11, 2014

Client Chemistry, Communities and Talent are the themes of today's *Monday Morning Mail*.

Upon my return from vacation I spent the last two weeks in many client discussions, a few pitches and in deep conversations with a number of staff. I met with many clients and we have healthy relationships with these clients and our work has been praised. But there is something more about these relationships that makes me very proud. There is very strong Chemistry between our teams and the clients. There is love. The healthy kind of love that makes working together a delight. In many respects it is hard to tell the difference among the client representatives and the agency teams. The meetings are not name and blame sessions, but how do we do things better, more quickly and more creatively, and what will it cost? These meetings make me feel energized about this business and our role in helping our clients. There was one meeting held, however, where we had an enemy in the room. It was a pitch and this person was lobbying for another firm. The jury is out on this pitch, but it just reminded me how important liking each other is to the client relationship. "Clients don't care how much you know, until they know how much you care," is a famous phrase from David Maister, well-known professional services management guru. In my view he couldn't be more right! We must make sure our clients know that we care, that we are quick to respond to their needs, and that we are constantly surprising them with love. If you are behind your desk everyday, that is a warning. Please start to count how many times you are on the phone with your clients and in their offices. I fully support our staff working inside our clients' offices. We need to be closer and "one" with our clients as we solidify our relationships and our business in the region. Thank you for all you do and will do to let our clients feel your love.

As I think more about what it is going to take in the next era of the marketing services business, I am more and more convinced success will come from sticky Communities. I truly believe if we connect more as groups we will all be better off. We have important client communities throughout the region, we have a growing knowledge community, brains community, new business community, Pacesetters community and more. We need to foster these. If you are working in a silo at Ogilvy you are missing out. We have challenges with silos and it takes people to just connect. So please think about how many people you connect with from different teams, disciplines and geographies and make a goal to increase that contact. It will help you and help us in the process.

My final message is one about Talent. Many of the people who have worked closely with me know that I believe the talent hunt and talent function are the responsibility of the leadership teams of each office. A person who does not handle client issues everyday cannot understand what type of people we need. The high-performing offices we have know where the talent lies in the market and they proactively court and cultivate this. We are encouraging each office to have talent plans consisting of what we must do to grow, recognize and stretch our current staff, and plans to understand what other talent lies in the market. Talent management cannot be taken for granted. It is something we must absolutely lead the market in and a discipline I hope we all model for the Ogilvy Group.

****

Getting people to hear you begins with mutual respect, September 22, 2014

"You can't save souls in an empty church" is one of David Ogilvy's famous quotes. I am not sure of the exact context in which he wrote or said this, but I would imagine it has something to do with the art of communication. Simply, in order to be heard you need someone listening. I thought about that a lot these past two weeks as I pondered the topic of "respect" and how important it is in our business. What has sparked this topic is a particular situation we are experiencing in Beijing. We are being put through a very difficult procurement process with one client whose finance team are just disrespectful. It is perhaps a negotiation ploy, but it borders on offensive and makes me wonder whether this client will be the partner we want to take us forward. The assignment is a big one and has the potential to be great so we are still in the game, but the discussions have made me think a lot about "respect" and how important this value is in our business.

First, I hope all of us at Ogilvy PR are respectful in every interaction with our clients and everyone we come in contact with. I hope we are confident and not arrogant, and that we are helpful, the best of service providers and fantastic trusted advisors. We are in the service business let's remember. We should delight in the fact that clients reach out to us for advice, and sometimes that will come at 6:00pm, and a lot of times that comes on Friday evening with a Sunday deadline. As long as the deadlines are not arbitrary we should delight in the fact that our clients need and value us. That's why they pay the hefty fees, and as long as they see value in our advice and support, such relationships should grow. But we need to set the climate for respectful relationships and if someone violates this, we need to politely let them know.

This weekend one of our teams has been working with a client who is being attacked by a competitor. Our advice was to be statesman-like in their response: to communicate openly and confidently and to rise above certain claims. They appreciated this and recognized that in doing so they will garner respect.

In my personal view, any form of disrespect cannot be tolerated. The minute we allow such behavior to permeate our company, it will become our own deadly disease. Also, everyone at this company deserves respect, from the tea helpers to the night watchman to the interns to the senior leaders. This is a behavior everyone must embody at Ogilvy PR and everyone deserves.

Respect doesn't start and end at work. It relates to our behavior in all parts of our lives. There is no special training for being respectful. What we need is just a little effort to consider what it takes to get people into the church so that a morsel of your sermon will be heard. Getting people to hear you begins with mutual respect.

****

Winning

Do you want to transform your organization or your team? Win a new client or an award for great work and the results will follow.

Chapter Nine

Winning

You don't win silver, you lose gold, August 4, 2008

Dear Colleagues,

With four days to go the blue skies are beginning to show in Beijing and we are in full swing.

I want to touch on a subject today that is very relevant to the Olympics. That is 'Winning.'

In my experience, winning is infectious. It is uplifting. Uniting. And it is confirmation that you are the best, or at least willing to go the distance, beyond anyone else to win. For us, we need to 'win' in our industry for a variety of reasons. To grow, invest, improve, attract staff, provide increases, give bonuses, and much, much more. In such cases, losing is not an option if we really want to be competitive here.

To me, winning in this business means we are willing to read more, study more, research more, brainstorm more, create more, provide more, service more, work more, charge more, explore more and make wiser decisions to distance ourselves from the competition. I believe as we enter the Games each of us should be asking ourselves this question: 'what length are you willing to go to in order to win?' In my experience, there needs to be some pain involved and only until we meet a certain threshold will we be ready.

This all may sound over-the-top to you, but to me, this determines success. Anything short is mediocre, and if you want to be mediocre, please do so at another firm.

So in this spirit, and as we gear up for the Games, and as I am feeling very competitive, I can only think about a campaign I saw years ago by a company that competes with our beloved adidas: 'You don't 'win' silver, you lose gold.'

This speaks to the opportunities that are in front of all of us in such a fast-growing market as China, and I hope we can all join together in the next five months and into the future to win a disproportionate share of the opportunities.

Environmental Tip of the Week

In the spirit of the Green Olympics, China is becoming a world leader in clean energy technology: About 16% of China's electricity came from renewable sources in 2006, led by the world's largest number of hydroelectric generators, according to the report. The nation's goal is to increase the proportion of renewable electricity to 23% by 2020. China invested over US$12 billion in renewable energy in 2007, second only to Germany.

****

Execution and fundamentals, February 23. 2009

Dear Colleagues

It's great to be back. Particularly to the onflow of new business leads in the pipeline. We have no less than 15 qualified decent opportunities that span all of our offices and this is a big positive amidst a lot of the sour news out there. The more I think about what we need to do to thrive this year, the more the words "execution and fundamentals" come to mind. There is no room for "tomorrow" in this climate as it is all about today.

Environmental Tip of the Week

Big credit goes to Diana Wang in Shanghai this week for providing the tip of the week. She wins a free lunch paid for by yours truly. Anyone else have something to share? From Diana:

"We found that we consume much more bottles of water after we own a car. It's popular here to have a dozen bottles of water in a car. To reduce it, we take a cup with lid and a bigger sized 3 litres of water instead. We successfully saved money, used less bottles and even saved gas (by carrying less weight) by doing this."

Keep 'small' in the way we do things and leverage our 'bigness', November 9, 2009

Dear Friends,

One thing that is wonderful about working in our profession in China is that the opportunities are so ripe and diverse. One of my friends once said about working in China, "you can have your best day and your worst day on the same day"... and how true this is.

This past week we had a lot of positive news. We're finalists in a sustainability CSR pitch that was very competitive. We received even more emails and requests about our Shanghai Expo capabilities. We got word from Unilever that our long-awaited corporate campaign will kick-off strategy development. We have some 21 new business opportunities in hand in Beijing alone. We also got word that a pitch that we were expected to win, we did not win, and it reminds us that we must continually put everything into every opportunity.

I was also told that due to our size and success, many of our competitors like to talk about us as being "big", with some negative connotation. Meaning, Ogilvy is big. Arrogant. Complacent. Slow. You must remember that when we are pitching for business, or dealing with outsiders that "big" has its advantages, but also its vulnerabilities. We must remember this.

The *Monday Morning Mail* is an effort to keep us small in the way we do things, and leverage our bigness.

****

Congratulations on Network of the Year win, November 16, 2009

First, I would like to share the release that has been sent regarding our win at Network of the Year. Congratulations to you all. Everyone was part of making this happen and this is recognition about how great you all are. I enjoyed a wonderful evening with the Hong Kong team on Wednesday... and a late night with the team. I received a lot of great suggestions about how we can even be a better and stronger network. So stay tuned. And, if you have a thought on what would make us better, feel free to share. We are all investors in the success of Ogilvy and what I hope for all of you and us is that you also get returns on such investment.

A feeling of greater optimism in the air, February 1, 2010

Dear Friends,

Wow! That is the one word that comes to mind after watching the combined Ogilvy PR/H-line team perform on Friday evening at the Beijing Group annual party. I am in pursuit of the video so that I can share this performance with the entire PR team. After a few years hiatus of taking 2nd place, PR this year won the grand prize. The judges were laughing, I even saw some tears. "So creative"... one of the judges commented.

There is a feeling in the air of greater optimism as we move into 2010. At least there are a lot of pitches and many new, exciting projects. We must just make sure that we get and convert a disproportionate share of these.

****

Need for all of us to accelerate our digital prowess, May 10, 2010

Dear Friends,

I am writing with a smile on my face and joy in my heart as I review how productive all of us were this past month. April was great for us and I have each of you to thank for this.

We should all congratulate the Shanghai team, who worked throughout the May holiday manning the more than 10 Shanghai Expo clients we have.

I spent last evening talking through all of our opportunities with Debby and they are plentiful. We have won a lot of significant new business this year. If there was one thing we believe we all need to improve upon, it is to bring more discipline into our day-to-day work. We spoke a lot about the need to develop compelling cases just after we finish these. And, to tease out the true value and insights we bring to every assignment. We also spoke about the need for all of us to accelerate our digital prowess. We will review the Digital Influence belts to see who is prepared to lead us into the new areas of marketing.

Looking forward, next week we will welcome Marcia Silverman to our markets and I hope everyone has a chance to get a dose of Marcia. She is truly inspirational and is responsible for how well positioned we are in the world. Please do reserve your time when you see the staff meeting announcements that are being prepared.

Hunger and renewal, December 6, 2010

Hunger and Renewal. These two words represent themes that I have been thinking about recently for our business in North Asia. This past week I was given the honor to attend the Ogilvy PR European Leader's meeting in Prague, capital city of the Czech Republic. Did you know we are the overwhelming leader in the Czech Republic? I met many of the Ogilvy PR MDs there and also many of Ogilvy PR's Global Leadership. Chris Graves, our Global CEO, introduced many new aspects of his storytelling module, and we learned about new Ogilvy innovations being rolled out called the DO Brief and Fusion. These two tools you will learn more about in days to come and they are parts of what I believe makes the Ogilvy Group the innovator of future brand management in the world today. Please watch out for both.

Why Hunger and Renewal?

Hunger because that seems to be a common trait amongst the offices and leaders I have met that lead the best businesses. They know that opportunity does not just flow to them... and they put themselves into the paths of success. Michael Law, who heads up Ogilvy PR in the US West is a model of this. He is a great friend and superb new business guy. Every time I see him, he asks about my family, about many of you who he knows, and then says, "so what can we work on together?" He has hunger like few I have met before. Andrew Thomas who leads our Singapore office is similar. He loves to talk about the new biz opportunities we are working on together. Both of these folks are constantly in search of new food (new business) and it is reflected in the health of their operations.

Renewal. There was a time when the Singapore office was barely performing. And our California operation was nearly sinking into the Pacific like the rest of California. But both Michael and Andrew focused on step-by-step what needed to be done to get them to the next level. Michael created the best public affairs shop in the Western part of the United States. Andrew has led Singapore to be amongst the leading public relations firms in the market.

In Prague Michael, Andrew and I had the chance to share views on what makes our operations a success with the European leaders. I do feel we have the hunger in North Asia, but what about the renewal? This is something I think each of us have to ponder as we enter 2011. What are you going to do to keep yourself fresh, relevant and competitive? And what obstacles do we need to overcome to achieve greatness? I don't think we need giant steps for any of us to get to the next level. We do need clarity, however, and a plan to get there. That is what I would encourage each of us to do in the coming days. People often ask me why I have so much energy after sixteen years in

China. My response is simple. I feel we have really only begun to scratch the surface of what we are capable of and, with the changing nature of communications, we are in a perfect spot to lead this change. Are you up for it?

In terms of office developments, one practice area to keep our eyes on is the Branding States practice. There seems to be a common theme coming across North Asia with opportunities to brand cities, provinces, regions and countries. This is true in all of our markets and we have a lot of experience in doing so. I hope everyone in the future will have an opportunity to work on a location branding campaign and please do reach out to me for information about what we are doing in this area.

****

Embrace 'what if' by working to challenge convention, January 24, 2011

Dear Friends,

What if...? These two words you will hear a lot about this year. They formed the theme of a meeting I attended last week with the leadership of Ogilvy PR in Asia, and they will remain a theme of ours throughout the year.

What if we really understood our strengths and weaknesses as a group? *What if* each and every campaign we launched significantly built the business of our clients? *What if* we launched our digital practice 10 years ago? *What if* we could attract, grow and keep the best public relations professionals in the market? *What if* we got paid what we felt our clients should pay us for our ideas? *What if* we had an incentive plan to pay people commensurate with their contribution to the company? And the "what if" list goes on.

You will hear much about last week's conference going forward but three things resonated with me that I would like to share.

First, the whole "what if" theme revolves around giving all of you permission to be creative, to try new things, to fail if that's what it takes. With this note, I am giving everyone "permission" to break the norm. I ask you only to work in the best interests of your clients, our firm and the people, but let's embrace "what if" by working to challenge convention, break out of the box and really be creative.

Second, the Ogilvy Big IdeaL was presented again. The Ogilvy Big IdeaL is that "Ogilvy believes the world would be a better place if we could bring out the inner greatness in brands, companies and people." This has deep meaning for me. The money we make is a by-product of bringing inner greatness out for our clients and our people and it is this ambition for me that is most exciting. Everything we do at Ogilvy should stem from finding the inner greatness in our clients, people and our firm and that is a noble undertaking. I would add our community to this and I hope everyone this year has the chance to work on some sort of pro-bono assignment in addition to your daily work.

Third, Ogilvy Public Relations' role in the digital space became much more crystalized for me. It is clear that leadership in digital will come from not only knowledge of the channels, but engaging "content." In some way we all need to morph into digital strategists or content specialists and there is a lot to do in this area so we have our work cut out for us.

I have added one section to the MMM and that is the "What if" Question of the Week'.

> 'What if' Question of the Week
>
> What if... during the Chinese New Year you took time to thank the top 10 people who went out of their way to help you in the Year of the Tiger? I don't even need to explain why I think this is an important "what if..." question to ask.

****

Winning

The team killed themselves winning this but they knew it was critical and they won, February 24, 2011

Dear Friends,

> ### 'What if' Question of the Week
>
> "What if your dreams really do come true?" I want you to know that I believe in dreams coming true and this won't happen in isolation. You need a plan. Do you have a plan? I woke up this weekend to see a note from Chris Graves, our Global CEO, announcing a win for the London office to handle communications around the Olympics for BP. The London office knows BP and its brands well. They did not know the Olympics well and imported this knowledge. They built a compelling team and offer and walked away with the business. This is huge and reminds me of our own experience during the Olympics and winning the UPS assignment. The team killed themselves winning this, but they knew it was critical and they won. There are many lessons here. What first came to my mind is adidas' mantra, "Impossible is Nothing." While watching the news of what has transpired in Egypt these days, I am also reminded of "Impossible is Nothing." If anyone does not believe in the power of digital communications, you have your head in the sand. This movement was amazing and will be studied in years to come. We have just begun to learn about this and it has millions of implications.

During the Chinese New Year my email box filled daily with new opportunities. We have no less than 30 new biz briefs in North Asia and this excites me immensely. When there is a lull I get worried, but this Chinese New Year was vibrant with opportunity for our offices throughout North Asia. Our colleagues in Japan are dealing with Japan outbound opportunities. Our colleagues in Korea, Taiwan and Hong Kong have also been very active.

So as we return and begin hopping along in the Year of the Rabbit, I am optimistic and excited, as there are tons of fun and interesting assignments that make me believe that once again we are in the right place at the right time in the right company. In the words of the management guru Peter Drucker, "The best way to the future is to make it happen!"

Engage, be specific and ascertain budgets, February 28, 2011

Dear Colleagues,

There is an English language expression - "when it rains it pours" - and I certainly feel like that at this very moment. I spent this past week in our New York and Washington, DC offices and the new business opportunities for us are flowing in. Certainly new business is the lifeblood of all successful businesses, and having no less than 30 decent opportunities across North Asia is a wonderful position to be in. I have spoken about these opportunities with many of you and we have a collective belief that deciding "what to do" and "what not to do" becomes all the more important. I also had a chance to speak to a few companies with whom we pitched and lost in the past. I wanted to learn what we did wrong so that we can improve. The lessons from the two conversations:

- You cannot take a brief, go silent, and submit a proposal. You must engage, engage, engage throughout (unless the prospect tells you not to), and ask the right questions. I learned from one prospect that they decided to go with another firm because the firm promised to put a person on the business in the US to help navigate their China experience. I pinched myself because I feel we could have done the same thing if we knew this was an issue. The client is just beginning their China entry and they want to be hand held.

- "Get into specifics"! We hear this often, but one prospect told me that we provided broad guidelines, but not specifics in terms of how we would accomplish something.

- "We went with a firm that was more in line with our budget" was what one prospect told me. This pained me because we tried to understand what their budget was, but they would not share this. I am not sorry we lost if this is the case, I just wish we knew what their threshold was. We really need to work to understand our clients' budgets - or even a framework - so we can ensure we are aligned to what resources they are putting together for an engagement. We lose a lot on "budget" and making sure we treat this appropriately and with the right sensitivity is important. I don't think we should be spending hours and days on proposals if we don't even have a guideline on what a client wants to spend.

The key for us now, moving forward, is to first and foremost take care of our existing clients. A strong foundation of healthy clients is always a great recipe for a successful PR operation. Next is to identify, win and close some of these new opportunities. And that is where we are at right now. So March is important and I am looking forward to this very much.

Winning

> ### 'What if' Question of the Week
>
> What if your client came to you with US$100,000 more to spend. They did not give you a brief. But they said, "you know our business, what can you do for us to help us win in this market? What should we do and how should we spend this?" What would you do? Think about it. Why not find a way to have a casual conversation with your client and dream a bit and share your views and see what happens. I'd love to hear us doing these things and to hear about what, if any, result in an actual assignment. In my experience rarely will you be punished for sharing more and new ideas. Of course, we must first be sure we are delivering on what they need, but going beyond the brief is usually a welcome opportunity.

****

Getting the Serotonin levels flowing, March 28, 2011

Dear Friends,

This last week I had an unusual amount of Serotonin flowing through my body. For those that don't know what Serotonin is... it is the chemical in your brain that helps maintain a "happy feeling." Here's why:

- *I heard our colleagues in Japan were all accounted for. What I heard was everyone was shaken, but they are fine and coming back to work. What happened in Japan is a real tragedy and there are still sensitivities brewing. You can do your part by contributing to the Japan Relief Fund.*

- *The new business opportunities continue to roll in. And we are seeing these across all markets. Doing great work for our existing clients and winning new assignments is the lifeblood of a great agency, and we certainly have the makings for this. The assignments are also very interesting and bring us into new areas which even excites me more!*

- *I met a new "GIANT" that was hired by Chris Graves and Kate Cronin. Peter Hirsch is his name and he travelled to China last week for a pitch. He*

> spoke to the staff and shared some very valuable insights on crisis management. We can win global crisis assignments with this guy and I am so pleased he is on our team. Bio attached.
>
> - *I stood beside Joe Zhou, our China Public Affairs VP, watching him perform his magic this past week. Joe arranged for one of our clients to meet the Premier of China and we received compliment after compliment for this work.*

...and the list continues. Yet, I want you to know that I am not delusional. Not everything is exactly rosy.

- *Throughout the last two weeks I questioned whether we really wanted half of the new business we went for. We even lost a global China Outbound opportunity that I felt was perfect for us. That was a big downer for me and sent my Serotonin levels crashing.*

- *We are facing a point in our development where we need to think hard about what we do... and don't do. Sometimes admitting that we are not the PR firm that does "cocktail parties" is important. We are not the travel agents. We are the content people. We are increasingly the "digital" people. We are the "influence" people. We should be the people that understand the brand world the best. If we want to climb the value chain, we need to make some hard decisions. And we need to do this while not taking us away or out of traditional opportunities that come our way.*

- *I continue to worry about the situation in Japan. As if an earthquake and tsunami was not enough, this nuclear issue is really troubling. The country needs our collective prayers and good wishes directed at them.*

What makes me most excited, though, is believing that what is next is going to be better than what we have experienced already. And from a work perspective, given our momentum, I feel extremely optimistic.

****

Significant development opportunities in Mongolia's capital, June 20, 2011

Dear Friends,

As Justin Knapp and I walked through the streets of Ulaanbaatar last week, I couldn't help feel excited for all of us in North Asia. Ulaanbaatar, the capital city of Mongolia, feels every bit like China 18 years ago when I first visited. There is an energy in the air that you can feel on your fingertips. We have been brought into Mongolia by a client and what is wonderful is that there are significant opportunities for all our North Asia markets. There is significant Korean, Japanese and Chinese investment particularly from Hong Kong and the Mainland. We will find an opportunity for Taiwan as well. Anyway, stay tuned to this space as you may see more about our movements in Mongolia in the days and weeks to come.

As I did our mid-year review we have much to be thankful for. Strong client assignments, a healthy stream of new business, some wins, and spots of really good work.

I must confess, however, that I do worry. I worry about how quickly we are mastering the digital move, how committed to creativity and effectiveness we really are, and how we are moving up the value stream in all areas of our business. I feel this is our leadership's biggest challenge and we are finding ways to move us up. I am hoping we can help define the new era of public relations, and we will need all of your help in doing so. I also worry as I had a very unusual week last week whereby I turned down "three new business opportunities" that either represented a conflict or were not in line with where I believe we need to spend our time. Everyone knows you don't grow by turning down new business so this is a cautionary trend. I believe "what you do and don't do as an organization are equally important" and I continue to believe this.

Let's make today the beginning of the new era of PR and please take time to think about what your role could be in making this a reality.

****

Celebrate winning, August 1, 2011

Dear Friends,

Celebration! We must find time to do this as a company, as a team and occasionally on your own as you reach certain milestones. No matter how big or small we become, we must not forget the "wins" that got us here. In fact, in the early days, we used to celebrate a lot. We must not lose that.

So why celebrate? Well, as I boarded my flight to return to Beijing from the US, I received a note from Miles about the Ogilvy group winning a much coveted global advertising account with a leading global consumer goods company, based in the Midwest of the US, and their brands are highly respected. The pitch field included 10 other agencies and we emerged the winner. This note was followed by one from Paul Heath saying that we won a major electronics company globally. Both Ogilvy PR Taiwan and China offices were shortlisted for the global PR News Awards; Taiwan for its work with the Taiwan Pavilion of the Shanghai Expo, Beijing for its Chengdu Pambassador's campaign. I am feeling very good about where we are. I am also always conscious that we don't become too complacent and there is much we need to do to raise our strategic, digital, and all around competencies. The message here is to take time and celebrate. The new wins and assignments will become our lifeblood and they will lead us into the future and let's take a moment to celebrate.

****

Leverage 'unfair advantage' to continue winning, September 13, 2011

Dear Friends,

I have heard from many people how busy you are. I always feel that being busy is a gift in our business, as long as you are busy with the right things. Busy should mean clients value your services and we are being pressed to deliver more. I realize it can be frustrating juggling a ton of things, but that is the sign of success. The challenge then becomes how to free yourself up to continually inform, educate and to improve yourself with whatever free time you have.

On the new business front I have seen smaller competitors of ours become very hungry. They are reaching out to our clients to offer more for less, they are doing everything possible to win and beat us. They are reaching out to prospects with much more regularity and their pitches offer up more research and insight than we have done in the past. I hope we all keep this in mind and none of us rest on our laurels. If we go for something, we need to be hungry and nimble and do whatever it takes to win. I often speak of "unfair advantage". And "unfair advantage" is knowing more than the next competitor, having better chemistry, a deeper network that can help our clients, and more, but we must be sure we have "unfair advantage" to continue to win.

****

Healthiest practices love their clients, love their staff and love their jobs, October 24, 2011

Dear Colleagues,

As I write this Monday morning I am feeling optimistic, competitive and protective. Optimistic because the new business opportunities continue to flow in, our client relationships are strong, and we have performed reasonably well during budget time. Competitive because while I think we can win anything we put our minds and organization against, we increasingly are meeting tough competitors along the way. Competitors who want to eat your lunch and mine, and we just cannot let that happen. Protective because I know of many cases where our competition is calling our current clients and asking for a chance to pitch for their business and it reminds me how close we should and must be as we close out this year. So lots to be happy about and some things to worry about. I cannot reinforce enough how important it is to get expectations and chemistry right with our clients. The healthiest offices, practices and groups are those I have found who love their clients, love their staff and hence love their jobs and we need to work hard to get everyone in the right place to continue to thrive.

****

Monday Morning Mail

Awards are the ultimate endorsement of what we do, November 7, 2011

Dear Friends,

Celebration and Renewal.

It is nearly a week since the Professional Achievement Award competition that saw Asia picking up 10 of 22 awards, with our North Asia team bringing in six of these 10. We need to celebrate and congratulate the Goodyear, Johnnie Walker and Chengdu Pambassador's team (2 awards) as well as Thomas Crampton and Daniel Ch'ng (also part of our team). And we need to say woo hoo and hoorah to the Chengdu team for winning best of show. The Shanghai office also won three Sabres last week, two for Goodyear and one for Cialis. It is such an honor and delight to be associated with you all and I am grateful for the global recognition you have brought to us. So thank you and please take time to celebrate. The awards are recognition our work is really great and I love these, but I love making clients happy and hearing that they have put their full marketing futures in our hands. This past week I learned that we have that coming to us in Chengdu. For me this is the ultimate endorsement and gift. In fact, last week the client from Chengdu volunteered to fly 10 Ogilvy PR executives to China in mid-December to make recommendations on what they should do in their dedicated countries/regions in 2012. This is true, genuine recognition.

There were other reasons to celebrate as well. There is a crisis client in China that felt Ogilvy PR was much more strategic than the firm they were using to handle a crisis and selected us. We won a few China Outbound assignments that are proof this practice is truly taking off. Guangzhou team made their tours around North Asia with Wines of Chile and I read a letter from the client that was very complimentary.

We certainly have reason to celebrate and I can't thank you all enough for how great I am feeling about the work of this network.

Yet real professionals take time to celebrate, reflect, spread the love, reflect some more and then move on. And that is what I would like us to do. We are entering the home stretch in 2011 and we are doing very well. So let's find time to celebrate and then focus on next year and what we must do to even better ourselves.

'What if' Question of the Week

So in the spirit of "what if?" what if we all take a moment to think about 2012, NOW, and how we want to improve ourselves?

That is the renewal part. We have done great with a few campaigns from China. Why not more? What about our work in Guangzhou, Hong Kong, Taiwan, Seoul, Japan? I am sure we have award winning work from there. What must we do to capture more awards from more parts of North Asia? And think how transformative life can be if your clients come to you and ask, "If we give you US$1 million more, what should we do?" One thing I know is that the more revenues we have in our offices, the more flexibility we have in taking care of our people. And that gets me excited. I feel that we are on the top of our game, but the game keeps changing and new players are entering the field. Are those new players joining Ogilvy? Can we compete with these youngsters? Are we getting "older" or "more experienced"? All things to think about during this period of renewal. People keep asking me if I am getting tired of doing this job after 16 years now in North Asia. And to be absolutely, gut-level honest with you, I feel I'm having the most fun I have ever had. I feel really good about our team and our work. And I know we can compete with the very best. So for 2012, my wish is for all of us to "up our game" and improve ourselves and the rest will flow naturally.

****

Like Olympians, we must be prepared to 'medal' every day, August 20, 2012

Dear Friends,

I spent the last several weeks in London at the Olympics. I love the Olympics. It is an event that brings together people of all nations competing in sport. The Olympics, for the most part, is an event where people forget about what makes them different and focuses rather on what is the common thing bringing them together. This common element is the sport in which they are competing. The significance of the Olympics in bringing people and nations together cannot be overstated. It is also a celebration of human potential. Athletes spend their entire lives in pursuit of a single-minded goal - to medal at the Olympics. And when these athletes take the medal stand it is very emotional. Personally, I love every aspect of the Games. The multicultural nature of the event. The sports involved. The athletes. The emotion around winning and losing. And the general atmosphere that surrounds this. And I love how it links to so much of what we do. I like to think we are in the sport of communications; bringing people, companies and institutions together through messages and engaging content. If we do this well, we win, by reinforcing relationships people have with the client companies we are representing. If we fail, we risk the chance to connect. It is like coming in 23rd. Unlike the Olympics that celebrates participation, for us participating is not enough. Our clients are paying us to succeed, because we are communications medalists (professionals) and we know how to make an impact. So if you feel pressure everyday that is good. It means you are in the game. If you don't like this type of pressure, perhaps this business is not right for you. At Ogilvy PR, we must be prepared to medal every day. Our clients are expecting this and I hope you expect this from yourselves.

****

Making your own luck, October 22, 2012

The topic for this week's *Monday Morning Mail* is about "luck" and what we must do to improve our luck in everything we do. Luck as defined by Webster's dictionary is "a force that brings good fortune or adversity." While luck is something that often happens by chance, I believe in the possibility of "making your own luck" and "improving your luck." Those people who are often considered more lucky than most, I believe, have a number of qualities in common that are instructive for all of us. These qualities include diligence and hard work, honesty, focus and optimism. Simply, lucky people I find go the extra yard, are straight forward, driven and very positive minded. They frequently succeed more often than they fail and they rebound from adversity better than most.

In many of our operations in North Asia we have experienced wonderful success. We can win when we want to and we have a great portfolio of long-term loyal clients. This is a result of the contribution of everyone in the North Asia region and our ability to make our own luck. While personally I can do better in many respects, I feel I am an extremely lucky person. And I have had my share of good luck this past month; first with the Holmes PR Award and then with the China PR Cover Story. I want to let you all know that I consider myself a very fortunate and lucky person and this is a result of the fact that I work with many of you. So thank you from the bottom of my heart for all you have done to put us in "luck's path" and for giving me so much "face" in being the leader of this company.

We need some luck in the coming months to finish the year strongly and I am feeling good that as long as we do what we have done thus far, we will be in good shape. With that said and in the spirit of David Ogilvy's "Divine Discontent" we have a long way to go in our leadership of Social@Ogilvy and other practices. We need to continue to be diligent and uncomfortable so we can put ourselves in luck's path as we enter 2013.

****

Importance of debriefs on both wins and losses, June 3, 2013

The Sweet Smell of Victory. One thing I know about this business is that a nice competitive win can be totally uplifting. And that is what I felt this last Friday morning when I was told the Public Affairs team in Beijing won a large government assignment for a major animal health company. This was a long pitch process that saw four firms compete for a strategic assignment. We beat the incumbent and we were told we really hit the mark in the proposal and the Q&A. We did almost lose this, though, as I was told our "presentation" on game day was not as good as one other firm. I have also been uplifted of late in Beijing by the Marketing team who won a number of luxury local fashion brands and by the H-Line Ogilvy, who I was told received a standing ovation from our client for a presentation we made. Public relations firms grow by farmed business from existing companies and winning new business. And in winning new business our company and staff are presented with new challenges that help us grow.

Most importantly it helps us carve out our futures even better by providing fees to help build our teams and pay our people. What also excites me about these wins is that we have properly evaluated them. We have worked hard to understand if they were real or not, and then we put the necessary time in to provide our clients with the right recommendation.

We did not win 100% of our opportunities, though, and I had a debrief with a client that told me we were about #3 in a line up of six firms as we didn't convince them we had the necessary experience to manage their business on the ground. Taking a debrief on both wins and losses is important and I have shared with the team the feedback so they know how to improve in the future.

****

Winning is infectious, November 25, 2013

Dear Colleagues,

Aloha and Amen! There is nothing that feels better than a well-earned victory and that is what we experienced in Beijing last Friday. Huge congratulations to Stephen Turner and his band of hula-dancers who - on the edge all week on whether or not we would win the four-agency duel for the Hawaiian Airlines business - flew away with the business. My congratulations to Stephen for his leadership and the whole team for bringing it home. And while Stephen briefed me on his win, Simon Webb smiled at me and reported winning an assignment with KPMG to write a sustainability report for a client in the FMCG category. And, all of this news came as I was walking into the office after a dinner with our Crayola client in Shanghai where they raved about the work of our Social team led by Jeremy and Bob.

Leading an agency that wins new and exciting assignments, and receives compliments for work delivered is a nice place to be.

So here I am writing this note to you on Monday morning excited about what this week will bring. And that is the message for today's *Monday Morning Mail*. There is nothing that energizes an agency more than winning a new assignment. It is the food that helps an agency grow. Yes, farming clients is important and that provides the grains and nutrition. But a win like Hawaiian Airlines to an agency is like attending a luau (a traditional Hawaiian party or feast) and getting drunk on a lot of fruit drinks. It's nutritious, tastes good and you walk around smiling for the entire evening. There is a lot of work ahead of us but the point here is that **WINNING IS INFECTIOUS**! The other great thing about this win is that I was told the chemistry with the client was great. Great clients deserve great work and that is what I am hoping for from Team Hawaii.

Healthy new business wins. Great chemistry. Energized people. Fantastic work. Social with data to support. Mix these together and what you get is a healthy and happy agency that arrives on Monday morning wishing that we could work eight days a week.

****

Losing feels like a bad hangover but analyse' loses' to assure future wins, February 17, 2014

Dear Friends,

Winning and Losing! With the Winter Olympics in full swing and watching the emotion of those who win and lose on the medal blocks, it is easy to witness how much is at stake for those who spend their lives working towards one goal. What is at stake, in many ways, is no different for all of us.

I have made "Winning and Losing" the feature of this *Monday Morning Mail* because these two words are central to how we will write our story of 2014. Simply put, if we win a disproportionate share of the opportunities in front of us, we'll have a beautiful year that sets us up for success down the road. Winning NOW is important because it literally shapes what we can do the rest of the year. Losing is important too. Losing shows we are willing to take risks, to put our "hat in the ring" and to stretch ourselves with new challenges. There is no shame in losing, but we must make sure the ratio of wins to losses is at least 3 to 1 or better. And we must not lose the big ones. What is most important is that we learn from each of our wins and losses.

There seem to be a few things in common about all of our wins. First, I can sense a degree of confidence, excitement and passion from the teams for each of the opportunities. In many, we simply went further than most of our competition. We brought the clients along in the process, sorted out all chemistry questions and we showed them that we could bring them into new areas. I sensed nothing was traditional about each of these. We had creative ideas that demonstrated to the clients how we would specifically execute the ideas. We got the money component right and we made the client believe the investment would deliver a valued result. Getting all of the components right is like a well choreographed dance/figure skating routine or football/hockey goal (choose your simile).

Losing feels like a bad hangover after a night where you mixed a bunch of drinks. The only remedy I have found for such an experience is learning what we did wrong and making sure we don't do it again. From some of the feedback I have heard, we lose because another firm gave specifics about how they were going to execute a plan; a competitor presented a more confident/convincing/engaged team; or we were too expensive. These are all very valuable lessons so that we can continually improve ourselves. I personally believe in "unfair advantage." We need to get ourselves into a position where we win the pitch before we show up. If you are part of a team that is doing one pitch after another with no results, please STOP and evaluate our process. One thing I hope we perfect is how to evaluate and condition an opportunity.

****

Celebrate what you want to see more of, October 6, 2014

Tom Peters, the well known management guru, was known to say, "Celebrate what you want to see more of!" So in the spirit of this belief, and given the accolades Ogilvy PR received over the past few weeks, this *Monday Morning Mail* is dedicated to celebration and its importance in our business. We must take time to celebrate and applaud superior effort when such recognition is due, while also staying true to the Ogilvy culture of "divine discontent."

No company can exist today without a proper corporate social responsibility framework.

Chapter Ten

Responsibility

Strategic corporate philanthropy after the Sichuan earthquake, May 19, 2008

As you read this, it will be one week since the horrible earthquake in Sichuan. Like many of you, I have spent the entire week assisting clients with their donation support. I feel terrible as I watch the images on television, honored to work with companies who have reached out with support, and proud that Martin Sorrell has offered to match whatever contributions we make. I hope you all join me in making some contribution. The whole topic about how to get involved is one that interests me very much. What is the right level of support? What is a company's intention? And what are people independently willing to do to help? While I don't think now is a time to debate this... these are all good questions to ask. I was speaking to Donald Tang in our Beijing office and I mentioned that in times like this you do things not for anything reciprocal, but because it is the right thing to do.

What is interesting in all of this is the rise of Corporate Social Responsibility and how it is becoming fundamental to the ways companies operate. No company can any longer reap the benefits without thinking about their broader responsibilities in society. That's a fact. So in the spirit of CSR, I read an interesting opinion piece last week written by Bill Gates on Strategic Corporate Philanthropy. Take a look and let me know your thoughts.

News of the Week

We were honored this week to have our global CEO visit Shanghai to speak in the Women's Forum Asia 2008 Conference. This is her second trip to Asia in two months. I had breakfast with Marcia and she is fully supportive of everything we do and amazed by the energy in our offices. I had a chance to walk her through some of the great work we are all doing and you should all know that we have a great supporter in Marcia.

Case Study

For those of you who did not see this case study at the China Business Summit, please take a look at the Johnson and Johnson internal campaign led by our Shanghai colleagues. This case shows real creativity and insight, is prized by Johnson and Johnson (evidenced by our video that beams from their offices) and has led to even more work. This is what we mean by "getting the work right."

This Week in Digital

Michael Darragh has pointed us to a new trend taking place in the US, called BrandTags. Take a look and ask him about this. I am sure we are going to see this more.

Environmental Tip of the Week

I think we all need to do something weekly to demonstrate our care for the environment. For this week, I would like us all to insist that beginning now we work to do away with the paper cups... whether they are Ogilvy cups or just regular cups... and insist on making sure the Ayi's (cleaners) do not use these anymore. I support the purchase of more glass cups so that we can begin to make our offices paper free. There will be more we are doing in these areas, but this is a small measure to take. And, if you are drinking at Starbucks, and you do not have to "take away" the coffee, get it in a glass. It's ironic Mr. "Toni print this out for me" is suggesting improving the way we use paper in the office, but I am intent to make this a practice and we should do this as it is the right thing to do.

I hope you have a great week, deliver hugely for your clients, make your bosses look good and support your colleagues in the process.

****

Responsibility

Contingency planning for disaster recovery, May 26, 2008

Dear All,

We're nearly midway through the year, one that has been defined by great expectations and a horrible tragedy. I hope each of you spent the last week helping your clients with their earthquake response. I had many conversations and our clients are looking to us for recommendations on their long-term response... so we should all be prepared for this. I also want to thank everyone who personally contributed to the response. One lesson I have learned is that the companies who responded quickly genuinely escaped public challenge and question. And it makes me think that in good times and bad we should be having contingency planning sessions with our clients to help them prepare for any type of disaster recovery. The coming weeks will be a good time to raise long-term contingency planning and you will be given credit for asking the right questions.

Environmental Tip of the Week

Building off of the request made last week to cut down on the use of paper cups, could I ask all of us to work towards double-sided printing for all documents we must print out. I believe two-sided printing today is acceptable for clients and we should work towards cutting down paper use significantly. And if you don't have double-sided printers in your offices, please let me know. These are really small steps that we all must take towards improving the environment.

****

Bank with a mission to bring people out of poverty, March 16, 2009

More this week on the topic of your personal mission in life. Do you know what this is? I certainly hope as busy as we all are, you have time to think about this. I was reminded of this topic this week when I sat in a press conference featuring Dr. Muhammad Yunus, Nobel Laureate, Economist and Chairman of the Grameen Trust, organized by our colleagues from Shanghai and Beijing. Mr. Yunus was in Beijing as part of a client CSR sponsorship and I had the privilege of hearing him speak privately to the Chinese government. He was very critical of traditional bankers, who he said are in business to just "make profit." He went back to his core idea many times, by saying his bank was devised with the mission to bring people out of poverty. And he set targets for himself to achieve this mission: to bring several million people out of poverty by 2015. Watching him, you could see he was driven, confident and focused on the mission of bringing people out of poverty.

The week was also dominated by preparations we are asked to make for our business in the next five years. To many it seems strange to be writing a five-year plan for our business with the uncertainties of this year. But, by stepping back and thinking through where our business is headed in the next five years, this can help us prioritize where we spend our time, effort and money. There is no question in my mind that our business will become more digital. And, I could not feel more confident by learning everything I have in the last month about Ogilvy's digital capabilities. The world will become more "green". We are launching a sustainability practice to meet this need. There are a lot of thoughts about the possibilities, and I feel a great sense of confidence that we continue to be in the right business at the right time in the right geographic location.

****

Conclusion

I hope you enjoyed the *Monday Morning Mail* as much as I have enjoyed writing these entries. This type of communication is a labor of love for me. I enjoy sharing the wonderful material and lessons that have been given to me, and I love the feedback that comes from the giants of the Ogilvy world who receive this. I am eternally grateful to them and feel honored to represent them throughout the Asia Pacific region. Team, thank you for all you do.

Onwards and upwards!

Glossary of Ogilvy terms, including companies and affiliates in the Asia Pacific region

Frequently mentioned companies and affiliates:

Era Ogilvy Public Relations
A Taiwan-based Ogilvy PR-owned second agency with specialist skills in technology, corporate and healthcare communications
http://www.eraogilvy.com

H-Line Ogilvy Communciations Co Ltd 西岸奥美
China-based Ogilvy PR-owned second agency network with specialist skills in technology, corporate, consumer and healthcare communications
http://www.h-line.com

iPR Ogilvy & Mather
Hong Kong-based Ogilvy PR majority-owned second agency specializing in financial, corporate and marketing communications
http://www.iprogilvy.com

Ogilvydo.com
An Ogilvy & Mather thought leadership platform designed to share the very best in marketing communications worldwide
http://www.ogilvydo.com

Ogilvy Earth
Ogilvy's specialist practice focusing on leadership communications in the environment, sustainability and community areas
www.ogilvyearth.com

social@Ogilvy
An Ogilvy Group specialist practice focusing on leading and fostering the very best marketing campaigns for clients touching all aspects of the evolving digital and social media environment
http://www.ogilvy.com/About/Network/Social.aspx

Glossary

Frequently used terms:

BBS
Bulletin Board System – online chat room, forum or classified advertising services offered by websites (very popular historically in China)

CMO
Chief Marketing Officer

CSR
Corporate Social Responsibility refers to companies taking responsibility for their impact on society and the environment in which they operate.

FMCG
Refers to companies/clients in the Fast-Moving Consumer Goods category

Fusion
Ogilvy's operating system - a collaborative planning tool from the Ogilvy & Mather network comprising a set of tools and methodologies that help client teams harness the entirety of the company's capabilities to deliver effective integrated marketing solutions.

IR team
Investor Relations team

PA
Public Affairs – used mostly in this book with reference to the public affairs practice or teams

The Big IdeaL
A concept based on Ogilvy's belief that the world would be a better place if the company can bring out the inner greatness in brands, companies and people.

TRC
Ogilvy's Talent Resource Centre or HR department
www.ogilvy.com.cn

TVC
Television Commercial